# Spanish Lies

A comedy

# Frank Vickery

Samuel French — London
New York - Toronto - Hollywood

# SPANISH LIES

First produced at the Parc and Dare Theatre, Treorchy, by the Parc and Dare Theatre Company on 12th November, 1991 and subsequently at the Sherman Theatre, Cardiff, with the following cast of characters:

| | |
|---|---|
| **Boy Miguel** | Richard Tunley |
| **Girl Lorna** | Kerry Stewart |
| **Woman Lorna** | Christine Tuckett |
| **Dougie** | Frank Vickery |
| **Man Miguel** | Kelvin Lawrence Jones |
| **Woman Regietta** | Lynfa Ackerman |
| **Girl Regietta** | Lorraine John |

The play was directed by Brian Meadows

# CHARACTERS

**Boy Miguel**
**Girl Lorna**
**Woman Lorna**
**Dougie**
**Man Miguel**
**Woman Regietta**
**Girl Regietta**

The acton of the play takes place on the terrace and bar of a very small hotel in Majorca

ACT I
Scene 1 Three o'clock in the morning
Scene 2 Later the same morning

ACT II
Scene 1 Later that evening
Scene 2 Morning and evening several days later
Scene 3 Forty-eight hours later

Time — 1966 and 1991

Other plays by Frank Vickery published by Samuel French Ltd

After I'm Gone
All's Fair
Breaking the String
Family Planning
Night on the Tiles
Night Out
One O'Clock From the House
Split Ends
Trivial Pursuits

# ACT I

## Scene 1

*The terrace and bar of a very small hotel somewhere in Majorca*

*The general appearance is very much rundown. The hotel is situated high up on a hill. There is a breath-taking view of the bay below as it stretches for miles into the distance*

*There are no more than four or five tables, each with a small umbrella offering limited shade. There is glass of wine on one. There are eight or ten folding chairs on the terrace. The actual hotel is R. There is a window and door on the ground floor, and two windows on the second floor. Each of the windows has a canopy but neither of them look as if they have worked for some time. The building was once painted a pinkish peach, but time and the penetrating sun have long since faded the original colour. Cracks, large and small, have now appeared on the facework of the building, and even small areas of rendering have fallen away revealing some of the stone work underneath . Although the property looks as if it might collapse into a pile of rubble at any moment, geraniums are in abundance adding to the overall quaintness*

*When the* Curtain *rises it's two, maybe three o'clock in the morning. There is a dim light coming from inside the ground floor of the hotel. The terrace area is mainly lit by the full moon. Small lights are twinkling on the far side of the bay. After the introduction music for the play, the lights fade to black-out. When they come back up Woman Lorna is sitting at a table far* L. *She is drinking a glass of wine and a cigarette. No music is playing now. All that can be heard are two waves crashing in the distance. After she drags on the cigarette we hearWoman Lorna's thoughts (with an echo effect)*

**Boy Miguel** (*voice over—almost singing it* )  Señora Lorna.
**Woman Lorna** (*voice over* )  Ohhh Miguel.

**Boy Miguel** (*voice over* ) Maybe one day you come back, eh?

**Woman Lorna** (*voice over*) Majorca ? Why would I want to go back to Majorca ?

**Dougie** (*voice over* ) It's where we spent our honeymoon. Don't you remember?

**Woman Lorna** (*voice over* ) Oh I remember ... I remember ... I remember... I remember ...

*Her thoughts fade. There is a slight pause before some very slow lilting Spanish music is played*

*Girl Lorna appears from the hotel*

*The second she does, Woman Lorna turns to look at her as she walks across the terrace. They actually look at each other as Girl Lorna passes to stand just behind. She takes up a position almost UC. She has her back half to the audience as she stares down over the twinkling bay*

*After a few seconds Boy Miguel, wearing a pair of shorts, a yellow vest and nothing else comes to stand in the doorway of the hotel*

*He is smoking and after taking one long drag, he notices Girl Lorna at the other end of the terrace. He throws the cigarette to the floor and steps on it to put it out, immediately burning his foot. He hops around for a second or two before returning his foot to the ground and making his way over to her. Reduce the volume of music although it continues to play quietly throughout the following short scene*

**Boy Miguel** (*almost singing it* ) Señora Lorna?

*Girl Lorna half turns her head then looks back towards the bay. Woman Lorna sips her wine as she remembers*

**Boy Miguel** Beautiful, eh? Beautiful like your name. ( *He speaks her name and relishes it* ) Lorna. (*A slight pause* ) You like beautiful things. Soon as you book in I tell. (*A pause* )You and señor Douglas like room? Everything OK for you?

*After a slight pause Girl Lorna nods but still doesn't turn around*

You have trouble to sleep? Too hot maybe — I put fan in room, eh?
**Girl Lorna** (*turning as she moves away* DS) A fan would be very nice, yes.
**Boy Miguel**  Ah señora she cry? Why beautiful woman cry? I do
something?
**Girl Lorna**  No, no you do nothing. (*She corrects herself immediately* )
I mean , you didn't do anything. (*She tries to smile* )
**Boy Miguel**  Then why you no sleep? You have problem, yes?
**Girl Lorna**  You're not sleeping either.
**Boy Miguel**  I have some hours and siesta. I no need sleep, you know?
(*Slight pause* ) Last honeymoon couple stay here I no see for three days.
No eat, no drink, all day make love.

*Girl Lorna laughs ever so slightly*

Why you no make love all night?

*Her laughter turns to crying*

'Tis very sad to see beautiful woman cry. Señor Douglas, he make you
do this?
**Girl Lorna**  No.
**Boy Miguel**  Then why you have tear?
**Girl Lorna** (*crossing in front of him* ) Doesn't your wife cry sometimes?
**Boy Miguel**  My wife no beautiful. (*He laughs* ) No, no I joke — I play
with you. I have no wife.
**Girl Lorna**  I thought Regietta——
**Boy Miguel**  No, no, no, no, no. Regietta ... Regietta, she no wife. She
cook, she clean, she serve paella, make bed, but she no wife. She work
... I pay.
**Girl Lorna**  She stays here.
**Boy Miguel**  She sleep in — have own room, yes. She good friend. (*He
moves towards her* ) You ... good friend? (*He puts his hand on her
bottom* )
**Girl Lorna**  To you?

*Boy Miguel nods and she nods back, smiling*

Yes ... yes why not?

**Boy Miguel** (*going out*) You drink with me? We share wine together?

*A light comes on in an upstairs room in the hotel*

**Girl Lorna**  A glass of wine would be very nice.
**Boy Miguel**(*going inside* ) Please. You wait. I go get. I be five minutes. You no go way.
**Woman Lorna**  I'm not going anywhere.

*Boy Miguel goes into the hotel*

*The two Lornas watch him as he returns inside the hotel. Spanish music swells but then suddenly stops*

*Dougie appears at an upstairs window. He hangs out of it as he looks down onto the terrace. He spots Woman Lorna and calls to her*

**Dougie**  Lorna? What are you doing down there?

*Girl Lorna begins to cross the terrace on her way off* L

**Woman Lorna**  I couldn't sleep. Go back to bed.
**Dougie**  Wait there, I'll put my trousers on and I'll be down. (*He disappears* )
**Woman Lorna**  (*calling after him* )  No! No, I don't want you to.

*Girl Lorna is passing behind Woman Lorna who knows her thoughts for the moment at least are slipping away*

Stay where you are ... I ...

*Girl Lorna exits* L

(*Almost under her breath* ) Oh piss off!

*Suddenly a string of Spanish is heard from inside the hotel. It starts quietly with a man and woman's voice but grows in volume until china is heard smashing—then it stops immediately*

*Dougie comes out on to the patio*

**Dougie** (*laughing* ) What the hell's going on in there then, I wonder?
**Woman Lorna** Sounds just like you and me, doesn't it? Only in a different language.
**Dougie** Couldn't sleep?
**Woman Lorna** Something like that.
**Dougie** I can't either.
**Woman Lorna** Makes a change from the last time we were here then. Honeymoon or no, you slept the entire fortnight.
**Dougie** I'm surprised you remembered.
**Woman Lorna** I'm sure that's why you wanted to come back, isn't it? Because you saw bugger all of it the first time.
**Dougie** I just thought it was a nice idea to bring your wife back for her silver wedding to the same place she spent her honeymoon. Most women would think that romantic.
**Woman Lorna** Most women would have enjoyed it the first time.

*They stare at each other for a brief moment. Dougie could pursue it further but decides not to*

*A slight pause*

**Dougie** So .... what are you doing down here all by yourself then?
**Woman Lorna** I was just enjoying being on my own. I was thinking. Reminiscing, that's all.
**Dougie** About what a terrible honeymoon you had.
**Woman Lorna** Oh it wasn't all bad.
**Dougie** Wasn't it?
**Woman Lorna** I made the best I could of it. I used to leave you sleeping on the beach while I went and did my own thing.
**Dougie** Which was what?
**Woman Lorna** Making love to any young passionate dago I could get my hands on.
**Dougie** (*laughing* ) Oh I love it when you talk dirty.
**Woman Lorna** Yeah, you love it so much you go to sleep.

*A slight pause*

**Dougie** I'm surprised he doesn't remember us. (*He nods towards the hotel* ) Old Miguel.

**Woman Lorna** (*picking up her cigarettes and lighter as she leaves the table and moves* DR )Well I'm not. I mean he must have had hundreds, thousands of honeymoon couples stay here over the past twenty-five years. Why should he remember us? Why should we stick in his brain?

**Dougie** He stuck in ours.

**Woman Lorna** Yours. I don't remember him now.

**Dougie** Well it isn't as if he was difficult to remember. It was only him, his father and that Regietta girl who ran this place.

**Woman Lorna** (*insisting* ) Look, I said I don't remember him. What's the big deal with you? (*More than a little peeved* ) He doesn't remember me——

**Dougie** — or me.

**Woman Lorna** And I don't remember him. End of story.

**Dougie** No it's not. Come on—think back. (*He goes to her* ) Don't you remember the time when you had ... er ... sunburn?

*Slight pause*

**Woman Lorna** No.

**Dougie** Yes. We'd booked to go to ... where was it now ?

*Woman Lorna mouths "Cala Bona"*

Cala Bona I think it was, and you couldn't go because you'd burnt the day before. I ended up going on my own. When I got back to the hotel you were nowhere to be seen. Apparently he'd taken you somewhere on his Vespa. I hit the roof until you explained you'd developed a couple of water blisters on your leg and he'd run you to the hospital to have them looked at. (*Slight pause* ) Remember now?

**Woman Lorna** (*dragging frantically on her cigarette* ) Vaguely.

**Dougie** When you got back your leg was in a bandage. It healed up very quickly though, because the same night you were up on the floor dancing with him.

**Woman Lorna** Bandage. Yes, now that rings a bell.

**Dougie** Well if you remember that you're bound to remember Miguel.

**Woman Lorna** All these Spaniards look the same.

**Dougie** No, he didn't, Lorna—and all the women knew it. It's a cruel

world though, isn't it? Because he's really gone to seed now.
**Woman Lorna** He hasn't.
**Dougie** What?
**Woman Lorna** Well...
**Dougie** Twenty-five years have taken their toll.
**Woman Lorna** (*moving to sit at a table down* R) I don't think it's been terribly kind to us.
**Dougie** I don't think I've changed all that much.
**Woman Lorna** Meaning I have.
**Dougie** I might have put on an inch or two around the waist, you know—gone a bit grey here and there—
**Woman Lorna** Here and there?
**Dougie** But on the whole I don't think I've faired too badly. (*He leans towards her with his hand resting on the back of her chair*) It's the sun that gets them in this country, you know. Twenty-five years in this heat will wrinkle anything.

*Woman Lorna doesn't say a word. Her eyeline is level with Dougie's crotch. She turns her head in its direction. Dougie moves away* DL

You're not bad for your age.
**Woman Lorna** Thank you very much.
**Dougie** No, you're not. I mean you've kept your figure pretty well and ... well your face doesn't have all that many lines.
**Woman Lorna** Shows when you looked at me last.
**Dougie** It doesn't.
**Woman Lorna** My complexion is like an elephant's arse! It's always been a problem for me.
**Dougie** It's never bothered me.
**Woman Lorna** It's not your face.
**Dougie** I look at it more than you. (*A slight pause as he goes to stand behind her putting his hands on her shoulders*) And it's not a bad old face really.
**Woman Lorna** (*putting her left hand to rest on his*) You like it that much?
**Dougie** Yeah.
**Woman Lorna** (*tossing his hand away*) You have it then.
**Dougie** Look, what is it? Tell me what's bothering you.
**Woman Lorna** It's this place. It's bringing everything back.
**Dougie** But that's the whole point of coming here.

**Woman Lorna** (*shouting*) I don't want to look back. I don't want to see what I haven't done in twenty-five years.

*She turns and goes to leave the terrace off* L

**Dougie** (*calling after her and stopping her*) I'm not dull you know. I'm not stupid. I know things aren't right with us and haven't been for a while now. But that's why I thought this holiday would help. Maybe make all the difference.
**Woman Lorna** It's never helped before.
**Dougie** We've never been in trouble before.
**Woman Lorna** Oh Dougie...
**Dougie** OK ... all right. I'd say things have been a bit scratchy for about six months. Nine at the most.

*Woman Lorna reacts. Obviously she doesn't agree*

Well, how long has it been for you then?
**Woman Lorna** Think in terms of a mortgage and you should come somewhere near the mark.

*They stare at each other for a second. Dougie turns and sits at a centre table. Woman Lorna sighs and moves up* L

*Suddenly more Spanish is heard coming from inside the hotel*

*Man Miguel steps out of the hotel. He has a handkerchief in one hand and a bottle of 'San Miguel' in the other. He mops his brow and drinks from the bottle before he spots Dougie at the table*

**Man Miguel** Ah señor Dougie. (*He goes to him*) You no sleep or you have woman trouble like me, eh?
**Dougie** I think I've got one because of the other, Miguel.
**Man Miguel** Beg pardon, señor?
**Dougie** (*for Woman Lorna's benefit*) I can't sleep because I've got woman trouble.
**Man Miguel** And I got woman trouble because I can't sleep, eh. (*He laughs*)
**Dougie** Sorry?

**Man Miguel** Ah, I toss, I turn, I keep her no sleep, you know? I tell her— make love to me. She say too hot make love. I say never too hot. What you say señor Dougie?

**Dougie** I say all women should be shipped to Formentera and us men visit them once a year.

*Woman Lorna turns and leaves the terrace off* L

**Man Miguel** (*laughing* ) Ah ... good idea but no visit once a year. Once a week maybe eh? Eh? (*He nudges him and laughs again* )

*Slight pause*

**Dougie** Your wife Regietta.
**Man Miguel** Ah ... Regietta no wife.
**Dougie** No?
**Man Miguel** No, no, no, no, no, no, no. She cook, she clean, she serve paella, make bed, make love sometimes, but she no wife. She work, I pay. Entiende?
**Dougie** Your father, then?
**Man Miguel** Papa? Ah Papa he — (*He gestures above* )
**Dougie** Oh I'm sorry. He died?
**Man Miguel** No, no, no, no. He live in room at top of house. (*He points to the side of his head with his index finger* ) He very sick man.
**Dougie** I wonder if he would remember us.
**Man Miguel** He no remember me. How he remember you?
**Dougie** You mean he doesn't know who you are.
**Man Miguel** I tell you — he very sick man. (*He makes the same gesture with his finger but draws a circle with it this time* )
**Dougie** Look, are you're sure you don't remember us ?

*Man Miguel takes a hard look at him and then makes a face because he can't really place him*

Hang on a minute. I've got something to show you. Sit down.

*Man Miguel sits down*

Now then ... what about this?

*He takes a photograph out of his wallet and shows it to Man Miguel*

**Man Miguel**  Ahhh, I know this man.
**Dougie**  That's me on honeymoon.
**Man Miguel**  Who is pretty lady?
**Dougie**  That's my wife.
**Man Miguel**  (*excited*) Aaahhh. (*Disappointed*) Ooohhh. She die your
    wife. You married two times, eh?
**Dougie**  No. No just the once. That's Lorna. That's what she looked like
    then.
**Man Miguel**  (*very surprised*) Señora Lorna? (*Slight pause*) Ahhhhhhh...
**Dougie**  You remember now?
**Man Miguel**  (*still studying the photograph*) Mmmm maybe, maybe ... I
    close eyes. Think hard, you know? Maybe I see her. You close eyes too.
**Dougie**  (*taking back the photograph*) I already know what she looks like.
**Man Miguel**  ( *shouting* ) Close eyes!

*They both sit with their eyes closed*

*Soft Spanish music is heard*

*Girl Lorna appears* L. *She is wearing a flimsy summer dress typical of
the latter sixties period. She comes and stands just behind Dougie's
chair*

**Man Miguel**  I see her. I see her.

*Woman Lorna appears from the same place as Girl Lorna. As soon as
she is visible to the audience Man Miguel speaks again*

No, I don't, I don't. I concentrate. Maybe she come back to me.

*Woman Lorna comes and stands left of Man Miguel's chair*

*As soon as she reaches it Dougie opens his eyes and sees Woman Lorna*

**Dougie**  (*to Woman Lorna* ) He does remember. I showed him this. (*He
    holds up the photograph* )

**Man Miguel** (*still with eyes closed*) Of course. Of course.

*The music fades*

**Dougie** (*to Man Miguel*) You know us now?
**Man Miguel** (*with eyes open*) I... how you say? I picture señora ... I have trouble with you.
**Dougie** Have another look at the photograph. (*He puts it back down on the table*)
**Man Miguel** (*looking at it*) I see so many.
**Dougie** I'm hardly that different.
**Woman Lorna** You've got to be joking.
**Girl Lorna** Look at all the grey hair.
**Dougie** (*to Man Miguel*) I remember you as if it were yesterday. You wore the same vest the entire two weeks we were here.
**Girl Lorna** It was yellow with a tear up the side.
**Dougie** It was green with a rip up the back.
**Woman Lorna** It was yellow and torn up the one side.
**Dougie** The left side.
**Girl Lorna** The right side.
**Woman Lorna** You don't remember him at all.
**Dougie** And you do I suppose?
**Woman Lorna** Now, yes.
**Dougie** (*to Man Miguel*) She's been insisting all along she doesn't know you from Adam.
**Woman Lorna** Well I know him now.
**Dougie** Since when?
**Woman Lorna** Suddenly everything is coming back to me.
**Dougie** I'll tell you when; since I got to remember you.
**Girl Lorna** You're stirring up a hornet's nest.
**Woman Lorna** You were very handsome, Miguel. (*To Dougie*) Your words not mine.
**Man Miguel** I change to you?
**Woman Lorna** Not a bit. You still look the same as ever.
**Dougie** That's a load of crap.
**Man Miguel** You too have no changed.
**Dougie** That's an even bigger load of crap. How the hell can he look the

same to you all of a sudden?

**Girl Lorna**  You're making him jealous.

**Woman Lorna**  I can see you now—

*Spanish music plays as Boy Miguel appears from inside the hotel and stands in the doorway*

*Woman Lorna goes over to him. He is wearing exactly what Woman Lorna remembers and this costume should be the same one as he was wearing in the opening scene*

—standing in the doorway over there in your little yellow vest  and shorts.

**Dougie**  I don't get any of all this. We arrived here yesterday and apart from me no-one could remember anyone. He couldn't remember you — and you couldn't remember him. Now all of a sudden everyone remembers everyone else but nobody and I mean nobody remembers me!

**Girl Lorna**  I can hardly forget you!

**Boy Miguel** (*almost singing it* ) Señora Lorna.

**Woman Lorna** (*looking up into his face* ) Yes, I can see you perfectly. (*She moves* UL *of Dougie and Girl Lorna* UR)

**Man Miguel** (*to Dougie as he remembers* ) You stay two week and you no want go home.

**Dougie**  Of course we wanted to go home. (*He goes* DR) We both did. (*He turns his back to the audience* ) Didn't we Lorna?

*The music stops*

*Woman Lorna doesn't answer him. She is still gazing up into Boy Miguel's face*

Lorna!

**Girl Lorna**  Oh God, I didn't.

**Dougie**  Lorna.

**Woman Lorna**  Yes.

**Girl Lorna**  Tell him the truth.

**Dougie**  You must be confusing us with some other couple.

**Girl Lorna**  Now's your chance. Look at him — tell him.

*Woman Lorna and Girl Lorna move to stand either side of Dougie*

**Dougie** (*turning to face front*) In fact we couldn't wait to go home. I was about to change my job and Lorna was really looking forward to moving into our new house, weren't you?

**Woman Lorna** No.

**Dougie** What?

**Girl Lorna** Good for you.

**Dougie** You couldn't have forgotten.

**Woman Lorna** No, I haven't forgotten. I hated that house.

**Dougie** What are you saying?

**Girl Lorna** Don't stop now.

**Dougie** We lived there ten years.

**Woman Lorna** I couldn't stand the place.

**Dougie** No, I don't believe you. We were very happy there.

**Girl Lorna** We?

**Woman Lorna** You might have been, Dougie. I never was.

**Dougie** Well if you felt like that how come in ten years I never knew about it?

**Girl Lorna** (*crossing in front of Dougie and coming to stand to Woman's Lorna's right*) You never knew about it in twenty-five years!

**Dougie** Well answer me.

**Woman Lorna** Why don't you work it out for yourself?

*A pause*

**Dougie** I think we'd better go back to bed, don't you?

**Girl Lorna** He's ordering you to your room.

**Woman Lorna** You go up — I'm not ready yet.

**Dougie** (*insisting*) I think we should carry on this conversation upstairs.

**Woman Lorna** (*equally determined*) I think I'd like another drink. If you want to go to the room that's fine. I'll sit and have a drink with Miguel.

*There is another slight pause in which Man Miguel laughs to himself*

**Dougie** No, look — I'll stay down if you want me to.

**Girl Lorna** Look, just bugger off back to bed, OK?

*A pause*

**Dougie** I take it you don't want me to, then?

*Woman Lorna takes one small step left creating a space between her and Girl Lorna just big enough for Dougie to walk through*

Fair enough.

*He leaves*

**Girl Lorna** (*more excited than worried*) Oh God, what have I done?
**Man Miguel** (*joining Woman Lorna* DR ) I go get something.....
**Woman Lorna** On second thoughts...
**Boy Miguel** (*joining Girl Lorna down front* ) No don't go. (*To Man Miguel* ) Stop her. Say something.
**Man Miguel** Vino.
**Woman Lorna** Pardon?
**Girl Lorna** Wine, you silly cow.
**Man Miguel** You drink with me.
**Woman Lorna** No.
**Girl Lorna** What are you saying?
**Woman Lorna** Yes.
**Boy Miguel** You will?
**Man Miguel** I go get.
**Boy Miguel** }
                    (*together* ) } You no go way.
**Man Miguel** }

*Man Miguel and Boy Miguel run off into the hotel*

**Woman Lorna** What am I doing?
**Girl Lorna** You're doing what you want.
**Woman Lorna** No, I'm doing what you want.
**Girl Lorna** Which is the same thing. You like him, don't you?
**Woman Lorna** Half of me likes him.
**Girl Lorna** Yes, that's right—my half.
**Woman Lorna** (*moving to the centre table* ) I know where it's all going to lead to.
**Girl Lorna** You want him in bed.
**Woman Lorna** Do I?

**Girl Lorna** You've only got to look at him.

**Woman Lorna** Yes ... but what about Dougie? I'm secure with him.

**Girl Lorna** (*joining her*) And that's enough? God, you're frightening me. I don't want that.

**Woman Lorna** It's not so bad. (*She sits*) I'm comfortable.

**Girl Lorna** But where's the excitement? You've got to have some fun in life.

**Woman Lorna** I don't think I know how anymore.

**Girl Lorna** Well, I do. Stick around and I'll show you how.

**Woman Lorna** You might do something you'll regret for the rest of my life.

**Girl Lorna** Better than not doing something and you regretting it for the rest of mine.

*A pause*

**Woman Lorna** Miguel doesn't really remember me.

**Girl Lorna** What difference does it make?

**Woman Lorna** It hurts.

**Girl Lorna** In twenty-five years from now it might, yes, but now who gives a shit?

**Woman Lorna** You will. I do.

**Girl Lorna** Look, I want him. I don't want to live the rest of my life wondering what it would have been like to have had him.

**Woman Lorna** And I don't want to live the rest of my life regretting that you did.

**Girl Lorna** Go to Dougie then. Remember though, what ever happens you'll regret it. Half of you is happy with a secure future, but the other half is going to stay here and wait for Miguel. You can't change anything because you can't go back, anymore than I can go forward.

**Woman Lorna** But I can remember, and you can imagine.

**Girl Lorna** Yes. And I do. (*She moves* DL) I can easily imagine my life here.

**Woman Lorna** But I remember a boring marriage so that kind of puts a stop on that, don't you think?

**Girl Lorna** Depends on who's in control.

**Woman Lorna** (*joining her*) Well I am of course.

**Girl Lorna** Now yes ... but I was then. Anything I do now has a huge effect on what you might remember in the future so I reckon that puts me in the driving seat.

**Woman Lorna**  At the end of the day you'll only do what I did.

**Girl Lorna**  Which was what?

**Woman Lorna**  It's all mapped out for you. I did what I did and you'll do what I did.

**Girl Lorna**  So what are you going to do now?

**Woman Lorna**  I don't know. I'm not as lucky as you, I don't have anyone to tell me.

**Girl Lorna**  I imagine that for tonight at least you'll go back to your hot little room and suffer in silence with Dougie.

**Woman Lorna**  Then—that's exactly what I will do.

*She turns and heads towards the hotel. She stops when Girl Lorna starts speaking*

**Girl Lorna**  See?

*Woman Lorna turns to look at her*

I am in control.

**Woman Lorna**  Yes. But only for as long as I can remember.

*Spanish music plays*

*Boy Miguel comes out of hotel carrying two glasses of wine. He goes straight to Girl Lorna but as he passes Woman Lorna she turns and watches him*

**Boy Miguel**  You like my country?

**Girl Lorna**  It's beautiful.

**Boy Miguel**  Your country beautiful too.

**Woman Lorna**  (*moving towards them* ) You've been to Ystrad?

**Boy Miguel**  Your country have you. You are very beautiful woman.

*Woman Lorna reacts as if he had said it to her now*

I have wife like you I make love all day, all night.

*Woman Lorna closes her eyes and relishes the thought. A pause*

Señor Dougie he wake no find you — he worry?
**Woman Lorna** (*encouraging him*) He's very heavy sleeper!

*All three are now standing together* c. *A pause*

**Boy Miguel** You like moon?

*All three turn* US *to look at the full moon. Boy Miguel's hand is on Girl Lorna's right shoulder, and Woman Lorna's hand is similarly resting on Boy Miguel's*

*General lighting changes putting Boy Miguel, Girl Lorna and Woman Lorna in the smallest spot possible*

I like moon. Moon very sexy.

*Boy Miguel allows his hand to fall down Girl Lorna's back until he is now touching her bottom. Woman Lorna repeats the move to Boy Miguel. Slight pause. Boy Miguel turns to Girl Lorna. The music stops*

You come with me?
**Girl Lorna** Where?
**Boy Miguel** To beach.
**Woman Lorna** What for ?
**Boy Miguel** Very beautiful.
**Girl Lorna** What for?
**Boy Miguel** Water very calm tonight.
**Girl Lorna** (*almost breathing down his neck*) What for?
**Boy Miguel** You unhappy. We talk. I make you happy for one hour. We swim in moonlight. I try make you happy. You come back, lay next to señor Douglas, he know nothing. Please. I go inside — get wine — maybe something to eat — we lay on beach have how you say—
**Girl Lorna** ——Picnic ?
**Woman Lorna** Sex!

*Boy Miguel looks straight at audience and raises one eyebrow*

*Very dramatic Spanish chords play*

*Black-out*

SCENE 2

*Morning. Breakfast is being served on the terrace. Girl Lorna is sitting at
one table, Woman Lorna at another. Both are wearing sunglasses.
Woman Lorna is looking at several postcards deciding which one to send.
Girl Lorna is doing the same*

*Girl Regietta comes out of the hotel carrying a tray. She puts one or
two things on it from surrounding tables*

**Girl Regietta** Señora finish?
**Girl Lorna**  Ah good morning.
**Girl Regietta**  Finish?
**Girl Lorna**  Er... yes.

*Girl Regietta puts cups etc. on tray*

**Girl Lorna**  I'm sending a few cards.

*Girl Regietta nods and smiles*

   How long will it take? (*She speaks more deliberately in order to get her
   to understand* ) How long here — home?
**Girl Regietta**  Five years.
**Girl Lorna** (*laughing* )What?
**Girl Regietta**  I come young lady. I help for one week — stay five years.
   I twenty-three now.
**Girl Lorna** (*laughing* ) I think we've crossed wires somewhere.

*Girl Regietta turns to leave*

   Regietta no, don't go. Stay? Talk five minutes?
**Girl Regietta**  Talk five minutes I stay one hour. Regietta very busy —
   dishes, you know?
**Girl Lorna**  One minute — that's all.
**Boy Miguel** (*off* )  Regietta, where are you, eh?

*Girl Regietta sits at the table with Girl Lorna*

**Woman Lorna** (*calling off*) Regietta? Regietta? What's happened to my
pot of tea? (*There is no reply . She calls again* ) Regietta?

*A string of Spanish is heard in answer to Woman Lorna's question*

> *Woman Regietta comes out of the hotel with a small tray, on which are*
> *tea things, in one hand and a well-wrapped baby, no more than a few*
> *months old, in the other*

*Woman Regietta bears little resemblance to Girl Regietta of twenty-five*
*years ago. She looks quite gross in comparison. Her hair is unkempt. She*
*is very poorly dressed in a very old and very well-worn black dress. She*
*has a pair of flat black canvas shoes on her feet with both heels trodden*
*completely flat where she has not been wearing them correctly over the*
*past few years*

**Woman Lorna** At last.

**Woman Regietta** (*angrily at first*) I very busy woman. Baby no sleep. All
do all day is drink milk and make smell. I no bring tea with smell. I clean
baby.

**Woman Lorna** If you're that busy with breakfast, why don't you give the
baby back ?

**Woman Regietta** How I do that? You tell how I do that.

**Woman Lorna** Just tell its mother you can't look after it.

**Woman Regietta** (*pointing to herself*) Regietta is mother.

**Woman Lorna** (*amazed* ) You are? You mean that's your baby?

**Woman Regietta** I have plenty babies.

**Woman Lorna** (*pouring her tea* ) How many?

**Woman Regietta** Sixteen.

**Woman Lorna** (*immediately putting the teapot down* ) Sixteen ... ? You
have sixteen kids?

**Woman Regietta** Ah no, no, no, no, no. I lose two, you know? (*She*
*crosses herself* ) Five live on mainland, twins two times, you know?
Seven marry, moved, live all over, one stay home, he no like girls — and
baby. Sixteen.

**Woman Lorna** Who would have thought when we came here all those years ago, isn't it? How long have you been married?

**Woman Regietta** Ah Regietta no marry. (*For Man Miguel's benefit who is inside the hotel* ) Father, he say he know if children his.

**Woman Lorna** He doesn't know? They do have all the same father?

**Woman Regietta** Of course. What think I am, sexy mad?

**Girl Lorna** (*to Girl Regietta* ) Five years? Why have you stayed so long?

**Girl Regietta** I meet man — I give my heart.

**Woman Lorna** (*to Woman Regietta* ) There's nothing wrong in that. You could have given him your heart but kept your legs crossed.

**Girl Regietta** But he no want my heart.

**Woman Regietta** He no want my legs crossed, you know?

**Woman Lorna** We all know what he wants.

**Girl Regietta** I love him so much I can't —

**Woman Lorna** (*interrupting* ) — Couldn't keep your knees together...

**Girl Regietta** He so beautiful —

**Woman Regietta** Then, I do anything.

**Woman Lorna** And now?

**Woman Regietta** Now he so ugly I do nothing. I lay with knees together and say, "Too hot make love".

**Woman Lorna** What happened there then? (*She nods to the baby Woman Regietta is holding* )

*Woman Regietta looks at the baby then back up at Woman Lorna*

**Woman Regietta** Oohhh we have winter in Spain too.

*A slight pause*

**Girl Lorna** (*to Girl Regietta* ) It's Miguel, isn't it?

**Girl Regietta**  } (*together* )      I lay with no-one but him.
**Woman Regietta** }

**Girl Regietta** Five year I stay. I think one day he marry me. I no want no other.

**Woman Regietta** Now I wish someone to come and take him. Thirty years I wait, he never say "Get married".

**Woman Lorna** You've told him how you feel?

**Girl Regietta** I no say but he know. He look. (*She runs her hands over her form* ) I tell. He like me but he no love me.

**Boy Miguel** (*off* ) Regietta, you come, eh? All dishes they wait for you.

**Girl Regietta** (*standing* ) He call — I go.
**Girl Lorna** Let him wait.
**Girl Regietta** No, no I go.
**Girl Lorna** I'll tell him I kept you.
**Girl Regietta** He make row — no like row. I go. I please him.

*Boy Miguel comes to stand in hotel doorway*

**Boy Miguel** (*trying to sound sweet* ) Regietta.

*He returns to the hotel*

*Girl Regietta takes tray and scurries off into the hotel after him*

*Another voice is heard from inside the hotel. This time it's Man Miguel calling to Woman Regietta who is still at the table with Woman Lorna*

**Man Miguel** (*off; impatiently* ) Regietta!

*A string of Spanish is heard*

**Woman Lorna** You called him ugly. You don't really think he is, do you?
**Woman Regietta** Inside he ugly. He no nice man. Outside ... outside he very sexy. Many lady love him. He love many lady, you know? Ladies who stay always lose heart. Very sexy man. They no like say no to him. I no like say no to him before, yeah? Thirty year it's OK say no now.

*Another burst from Man Miguel from inside*

**Man Miguel** (*off; more impatiently* ) Regietta! ! ! ( *More Spanish ending with the English* ) Who has seen fat cow?

*He comes out of the terrace and stops mid-sentence on seeing Woman Regietta sitting with Woman Lorna*

(*Very charming* ) Ahhh Regietta. Please, come inside. Need to ... er, to slice fat cow for dinner, eh?

*Woman Regietta and Man Miguel enter into what sounds like a very heated argument at the end of which Woman Regietta stands*

**Woman Lorna**  What did you tell him?
**Woman Regietta**  I tell him I go inside and maybe slice fat pig.

*She hits him on the stomach with the tray as she goes inside the hotel*

*Man Miguel is about to follow her when Woman Lorna calls after him*

**Woman Lorna**  Er... Miguel?

*He stops and turns to look at her*

Could I have a word?
**Man Miguel**  Please — five minute, eh? I very busy. Five minute OK—
have plenty time.

*He goes into hotel*

*As he goes in Boy Miguel comes out and goes straight over to Girl Lorna*

*She hasn't seen him approach. In order to get her to look up at him he throws a packet of cigarettes and a box of matches down on the table*

**Boy Miguel**  ( *leaning towards her with one leg on a chair* ) You like last
night?

*Girl Lorna smiles and nods*

We do again, maybe?

*Girl Lorna doesn't answer*

I like take to secret place.
**Girl Lorna**  Where?
**Boy Miguel**  I tell—no secret.

*Woman Lorna takes out a cigarette*

We go all day—you fix with husband, eh?

*Girl Lorna doesn't reply. She just stares at him*

*He reaches for a cigarette and offers Girl Lorna one*

You smoke? (*Before she has time to answer he speaks again* ) No, no, no, I forget. You no smoke ...

*Looking into his eyes Girl Lorna takes the packet from him and puts a cigarette into his mouth. Then she strikes a match and lights it for him*

**Boy Miguel** (*dragging on a cigarette* ) Gracias.
**Girl Lorna** Every time I strike a match from now on I'll think of you.

*Woman Lorna strikes a match to light her cigarette*

**Boy Miguel** Please—you come with me ?

*Girl Lorna nods*

When?
**Girl Lorna** Today.
**Boy Miguel** Today Dougie say you both go to Cala Bona.
**Girl Lorna** You just leave Dougie to me.

*Dougie comes out onto the terrace having just got up from bed. He is wearing a coloured short sleeve shirt, knee length shorts and sandals. He carries a camera in a case*

**Dougie** (*to Woman Lorna* ) Morning. (*He spots the tea things on the table*) I see you've eaten, then.
**Woman Lorna** I've had a cup of tea. That's all I wanted.
**Dougie** (*really put out* ) Well I wonder if I can get something to eat now.
**Woman Lorna** Hang on half an hour and you'll probably get lunch.
**Dougie** Lunch? Are you going to start now first thing in the morning? I slept on that's all and I don't know what you're going on about — anyway I was down here until God knows what time last night. I don't know what time you came to bed but it was well after me so I'm

surprised you didn't sleep on this morning too.

**Woman Lorna** Perhaps I didn't go back to bed at all.

**Dougie** (*slight pause*) Well bully for you. Strike lucky did we? Mind you if you did I'm curious to find out who with. There's no bugger here. Well nobody except a fat greasy waiter and his geriatric father who's confined to the attic. Look, I know you didn't score last night right, so let's just leave it at that. OK?

**Woman Lorna** (*slight pause*) Fine.

**Dougie** Good. (*He takes a brochure out of his shirt pocket*) Right. Now what are we going to do today?

**Woman Lorna** We did say we'd do the Caves of Drach.

**Dougie** (*sarcastically*) Then the Caves of Drach it is, my darling.

*Man Miguel comes out of the hotel and goes to Woman Lorna's table*

**Man Miguel** I so sorry. We have problem in kitchen. Regietta she get so big we no have room, you know? Something need to go, she say small table, I say 'her'. Need smaller Regietta.. Someone with bones, eh? Eh? (*He laughs. Slight pause*) Señora Lorna, she want me?

**Woman Lorna** No.

**Man Miguel** You call I say five minutes.

**Woman Lorna** No...

**Man Miguel** You ask for word.

**Woman Lorna** No.

**Man Miguel** You no want word?

**Woman Lorna** No.

**Man Miguel** Miguel he no make mistake. You forget or change mind, eh? No matter. You remember I no far. I only in kitchen. I ... move small table.

*Man Miguel goes back inside the hotel*

*Dougie pours himself a cup of tea and sits*

**Dougie** What's the tea like here?

**Girl Lorna** (*still to Boy Miguel*) I wonder what it'll be like twenty-five years from now.

**Woman Lorna** Bloody awful.

**Boy Miguel** Maybe come back, eh?

**Girl Lorna**  You ask me nicely and I might not even go.

**Boy Miguel** (*laughing* ) You joke, yeah? (*He laughs again then stops abruptly* )

**Girl Lorna**  Did I frighten you?

**Boy Miguel**  Señor Dougie he good man. He take care of you. You have good life together, he make you happy for long time. Me? Me I make you happy for one hour.

**Girl Lorna**  You made me so happy last night I'm going to be miserable the rest of my life.

**Boy Miguel**  But you will forget. That I promise.

*Girl Lorna smiles at him, not at all sure of what he is saying*

**Girl Lorna**  And will you ... forget?

**Boy Miguel**  Part of magic of island. Mallorca very special very, how you say ... precious land.

**Girl Lorna**  That's the most beautiful load of crap I've ever heard.

**Boy Miguel**  Crap? What is crap?

**Girl Lorna**  Of course you'll forget. As soon as the next load of tourists hit the tarmac you'll forget, but do you know, I don't care? I don't care because all that matters is now. I'm going to love now and pay later.

**Boy Miguel** (*outraged* ) No! No, no, you no pay! You no pay now or you no pay later.

**Girl Lorna** (*laughing* ) No, you didn't understand.

**Boy Miguel**  I never charge. I always give it free.

*Girl Lorna laughs hysterically. Boy Miguel doesn't understand what she is laughing at but eventually joins her with a smile. The laughter subsides and there is a special moment between them*

**Boy Miguel**  Many year from now maybe you come back. I look to see same love in eye.

**Girl Lorna**  Wouldn't it be nice if I see it in yours too.

*Girl Regietta comes out of the hotel and looks on*

**Boy Miguel** (*pause* ) I go now. I go make ready surprise. You sure señor Dougie he no make problem?

**Girl Lorna**  You go and do what you've got to do.

*Boy Miguel turns to leave, sees Girl Regietta and rushes off past her. She storms off after him*

*Girl Lorna stands and moves slightly towards Dougie who has his eyes closed*

**Girl Lorna** Dougie?

*Dougie opens his eyes*

**Dougie** Oh ...did I drop off?
**Woman Lorna** Don't you always?
**Girl Lorna** (*sitting on Dougie's left*) I don't feel very well.
**Dougie** Ah what's the matter?.
**Woman Lorna** I've just had a funny turn.
**Girl Lorna** I think it's the heat.
**Dougie** I've told you you spend too much time in it.
**Girl Lorna** I'm going to give Cala Bona a miss I think.
**Woman Lorna** Are you listening to me?
**Dougie** Yes. (*To Girl Lorna*) Well perhaps we can go tomorrow then— I wouldn't want to miss it.
**Woman Lorna** Look, I don't mind you going to the caves on your own.
**Dougie** But I don't want to go by myself.
**Girl Lorna** No, I want you to.
**Dougie** But I want you to see them too.
**Girl Lorna** Take some photographs. I have to settle for that.
**Dougie** (*to Girl Lorna*) If you're not feeling very well I'm not sure I should leave you on your own.
**Woman Lorna** I'm just having one of my migraines, that's all.
**Girl Lorna** (*getting up and standing behind her chair*) I'll go and lie down for a couple of hours. If I feel better later on I'll come and meet you off the boat.
**Dougie** It's not going to be much fun on my own.
**Woman Lorna** (*getting up and standing behind her chair*) You'll enjoy it far more than hanging around me. I'm going to ask Miguel to give me something ... then hopefully I'll be all right for tonight.
**Dougie** Why, what's happening tonight?
**Woman Lorna** It's cabaret, isn't it?

**Girl Lorna** I've definitely had too much sun. I'm burning up.
**Dougie** Are you sure you'll be all right on your own?
**Woman Lorna** ⎫
**Girl Lorna** ⎬  (*together*)  Yes!
**Dougie** Do you know something?

*Both women freeze*

I think I'm having *déjà-vu* here.
**Woman Lorna** ⎫
**Girl Lorna** ⎬  (*together*)  Why?
**Dougie** I'm sure all this has happened before.
**Girl Lorna** Don't be silly.
**Dougie** I'm telling you. I've said it all before.
**Woman Lorna** What here, on this terrace?
**Dougie** Yes.
**Girl Lorna** Strange, because you haven't been to Spain before.
**Woman Lorna** Perhaps you said something similar when you were last here.
**Dougie** Maybe.
**Girl Lorna** Anyway, shouldn't you be going?
**Woman Lorna** You don't want to miss your——
**Girl Lorna** —Boat.
**Woman Lorna** Coach.
**Dougie** Are you sure about this?
**Girl Lorna** You don't have to go if you don't want to.
**Woman Lorna** I don't want you to think I'm pushing you into this.
**Dougie** What time is it now ?
**Woman Lorna** It's quarter to ——
**Girl Lorna** —Nine.
**Woman Lorna** The coach leaves on the hour. Leave now and you'll just make it.
**Girl Lorna** Don't forget the camera.
**Dougie** (*standing* ) Right.
**Woman Lorna** See you when you get back then.
**Dougie** Yes. I shouldn't be long. It's only a half-day.
**Girl Lorna** No, no, it's a full day.
**Dougie** Are you sure?
**Girl Lorna** With a bit of luck I'll be there to meet you at four.

**Dougie** (*to Girl Lorna* ) All right then. (*He kisses Girl Lorna* )
**Girl Lorna**  Have a nice time.
**Dougie**  I'll try.
**Woman Lorna**  You go and enjoy yourself. ( *She offers her cheek for him to kiss it* )
**Dougie**  (*completely ignoring her offer* ) Yeah,  hope so.

*They both wave him off as he disappears* L

*A pause*

**Woman Lorna**  (*to Girl Lorna* ) Well, you've done it.
**Girl Lorna**  Yes.
**Woman Lorna**  How do you feel?
**Girl Lorna**  You should know.
**Woman Lorna**  Remind me.
**Girl Lorna**  A shit.
**Woman Lorna**  That's right. What are you going to do now?
**Girl Lorna** (*going to sit at a table far* R ) As if you didn't know. I'm going off for a surprise with Miguel.
**Woman Lorna**  It's no surprise he took you on his boat to his 'secret' place. It's a very secluded cove.
**Girl Lorna**  And you?
**Woman Lorna**  (*sitting at the table with her* )  Me? Me, I'm going to try and find out if it was all a waste of time.
**Girl Lorna**  It's not fair. Why can't I just have him and then you forget all about it?
**Woman Lorna**  Why can't you imagine what it would be like and leave it at that?

*She doesn't answer*

You've got to believe me when I tell you that once you've done it you're never going to forget him.
**Girl Lorna** (*slight pause* ) Will there be repercussions?
**Woman Lorna**  You mean will Dougie find out?

*Girl Lorna nods*

No, he doesn't suspect a thing.
**Girl Lorna** So I get away scot-free?
**Woman Lorna** Oh, no you'll pay. Believe me you'll pay.
**Girl Lorna** How? Tell me how?
**Woman Lorna** (*getting up from the table and moving* UC) When you get back home you'll be pregnant.
**Girl Lorna** Not by Miguel?
**Woman Lorna** You'll never know. But you'll want it to be his. You'll name him Michael too. Michael, English for——
**Girl Lorna** —Miguel. What will Dougie think?
**Woman Lorna** Nothing. He never doubts it's his. (*She opens her bag and takes out a photograph* ) But that baby, that little boy, that young man keeps things burning. For twenty-five years he's kept things burning.

*She hands the photograph to Girl Lorna*

That's Michael.
**Girl Lorna** I've just thought. If I don't go off with Miguel today Michael might never be born.
**Woman Lorna** But if you don't go and he is ... at least I'll know who his father is.
**Girl Lorna** Is that why you don't want me to go?
**Woman Lorna** I don't want you to go for us. I love Michael, he's very special to me, but if I could have my chance all over again with Miguel, I'd tell him where to get off.
**Girl Lorna** I don't think so.
**Woman Lorna** So what are you hanging around here for then? Go and get ready, he'll be here to fetch you in a minute.
**Girl Lorna** I don't know what to wear.
**Woman Lorna** You'll wear your lemon print dress with a pattern on the bodice.
**Girl Lorna** Boy, what a memory.
**Woman Lorna** I told you it was good. I've still got a photo of me wearing it. Miguel is going to take it later on this morning.
**Girl Lorna** How can he—Dougie's got the camera.
**Woman Lorna** I'm not going to tell you everything. Go on — enjoy yourself before you forget how.

*The two Lornas stand facing each other. They give each other a wry smile*

*Girl Lorna exits into the hotel leaving Woman Lorna alone on the
terrace*

*She holds the moment before taking out a cigarette from the packet
which is on the table. She puts it in her mouth, lights it and drags on it
thoughtfully. After a moment as she fans herself in the baking heat*

*Man Miguel steps out onto the terrace. He smiles as he eyes her up. He
pushes the hair back behind his ears with his fingers*

**Man Miguel**  Ahh señora. (*He goes to her* ) She remember now?
**Woman Lorna**  What's more to the point Miguel ... do you remember?
**Man Miguel**  Señora, beg pardon—Miguel he no understand.
**Woman Lorna**  It's me, Miguel.
**Man Miguel**  Señora?
**Woman Lorna**  Lorna. Miner's fortnight nineteen sixty-six.
**Man Miguel**  Sí, sí — I remember. Look, I keep photo. (*He takes out his
wallet from his rear trouser pocket*)
**Woman Lorna**  (*terribly flattered* ) You have a photograph of me?
**Man Miguel**  And me also. We are together.
**Woman Lorna**  And you've kept it all these years.
**Man Miguel**  Always. I never destroy. I keep next to my heart.
**Woman Lorna**  What do you take me for Miguel, you took it from your
back pocket.
**Man Miguel**  Only sometimes I keep there. (*He hands the photograph to
Woman Lorna. As he does this he takes a sly look over his shoulder
towards the hotel* )
**Woman Lorna**  (*looking at the photograph* ) God I look different.
**Man Miguel**  You no change. You still look like lady in photo. Every time
make love I think only of you ... of lady in photo ... of time we spend
locked together in sixty-nine.
**Woman Lorna**  Sixty-six.
**Man Miguel**  No, no ... sixty-nine.
**Woman Lorna**  Can I keep this?
**Man Miguel**  Why you want?
**Woman Lorna**  I've got a photograph too. One of us together as well.
We'll swap.
**Man Miguel**  How you mean, 'swap'?

**Woman Lorna** We'll give it to each other.
**Man Miguel** No, no, no. Later... when siesta. Regietta she sleep with little
one. I come to room and we, how you say, 'swap'?
**Woman Lorna** I'll show it to you.

*She crosses* R, *sits at the table and takes the photograph from her bag.
Man Miguel joins her at the table*

It's in my bag.Wait a minute and I'll get it. I've had to hide it from
Dougie. (*She finds it and hands it to him* )
**Man Miguel** (*looking at it* ) Miguel and Lorna.
**Woman Lorna** It's written on the back, look. ( *She turns it over for him
and reads it* ) "Me and Miguel — August sixty-six"
**Man Miguel** (*slight pause* ) Very good. Very nice, yes. (*Slight pause* )
Maybe I have own photo back now, eh?
**Woman Lorna** What?
**Man Miguel** Please ? I keep own photo.
**Woman Lorna** Can't I have it?
**Man Miguel** Very special, you know? I keep long time.
**Woman Lorna** (*slight pause* ) Well if it means that much ... (*She holds
it out to him then takes it back to have another look at it. Something
doesn't look right about it this time. She has a close look before turning
it over to see if there is anything written on the back of it. There is* ) Hang
on a minute. (*She reads it* ) "To Miguel. Many thanks for giving me such
a wonderful time, love Lena."
**Man Miguel** No, no ... Lorna, sí. (*He points to it* ) Lorna.
**Woman Lorna** (*spelling it* ) L- E - N - A doesn't spell Lorna. Not even
in Spanish.
**Man Miguel** You make mistake. Writing not very clear, you know?
**Woman Lorna** I can read September clearly enough — I was here in
August.

*She hands it back to him before getting up and moving* DR

So ... you don't remember me after all. I kept saying to Dougie all the
time.
**Man Miguel** (*joining her* ) No, no, no, no, no, no. I do remember you. You
are girl of dreams. (*Slight pause* ) I just keep wrong photo, that's all.
**Woman Lorna** (*laughing* ) Oh Miguel, you're awful.

**Man Miguel** (*insisting* ) 'Tis true.

**Woman Lorna** (*imitating him* ) I know 'tis true.

**Man Miguel** What's photo anyway, eh? (*He rips it up* ) There — I tear. You are one I remember. You are woman of dreams. We make love later, eh?

**Woman Lorna** Regietta.

**Man Miguel** (*surprised* ) Where? (*He looks over his shoulder* )

*Girl Lorna comes out of the hotel dressed in the lemon print dress that was earlier described. She hangs around at the back of the terrace waiting for Boy Miguel to meet her*

**Woman Lorna** You're very nervous.

**Man Miguel** No, no I think she creep up, you know? She always creep up. She very creep up woman.

**Woman Lorna** Maybe she has cause to be Miguel. You're a very 'creep up' man.

*Woman Regietta leans out of an upstairs window to shake a duster. She spots Man Miguel and Woman Lorna on the terrace. She stretches to look and listen*

**Man Miguel** She watch all time. I feel eye, you know? I no do what I want.

**Woman Lorna** Come on. You've always done what you want. You've got sixteen children.

**Man Miguel** I no have sixteen children.

**Woman Lorna** You don't?

**Man Miguel** I have one ... but they no prove, you know.

**Woman Lorna** Regietta told me she had sixteen children.

**Man Miguel** Regietta have sixteen, I two maybe.

**Woman Lorna** You just said , you only had one.

**Man Miguel** Three at most. (*Very insistent* ) But all no prove, you know?

**Woman Lorna** (*laughing* ) So who's the father of Regietta's children?

*He gestures he hasn't the faintest idea*

**Man Miguel** I tell you, she very creep up woman.

*Woman Lorna laughs and walks up to the hotel and stands on the first*

*step of the forecourt. Man Miguel follows her. They are both out of
view now from Woman Regietta who is still half hanging out of the
window. She immediately disappears back inside*

*A Vespa motor-cycle is heard pulling up and tooting its feeble horn.
Girl Lorna hears it and knows it's for her*

*She runs off to meet Miguel*

*As she does this Girl Regietta appears from behind the hotel. She has
obviously been watching her. She scurries across the terrace after her
and exits*

**Woman Lorna** So ... where is Regietta now?
**Man Miguel** I tell her make beds, change sheets, clean shower. She very
busy for long time. (*Slight pause* ) Señor Dougie?
**Woman Lorna** He's gone to the Caves of Drach. We won't see hm for
a while.
**Man Miguel** You like to 'swap' now?
**Woman Lorna** Pardon?
**Man Miguel** Not here. I have secret place. I take you there?
**Woman Lorna** It's not a secret , Miguel. I've already been there.
**Man Miguel** You have?
**Woman Lorna** Twenty-five years ago. I still remember if you don't.
**Man Miguel** Of course I remember. I just forget you remember. You
come now eh?
**Woman Lorna** I want to come with you. But I don't know if it's still there.
**Man Miguel** Of course still there. I go last week, still there.

*Woman Lorna laughs. He takes her hand and they begin to walk
across the terrace*

**Woman Lorna** You told me once you hoped I'd come back, do you
remember?
**Man Miguel** Of course. We were on beach.
**Woman Lorna** No, we were sitting over there. (*She nods in the direction
of Girl Lorna and Boy Miguel's last scene at the table* )
**Man Miguel** That's right. I say, ' I always hope to see same love in eyes.'
**Woman Lorna** (*stopping in amazement* ) You do remember.

**Woman Lorna** (*stopping in amazement*) You do remember.

*Man Miguel is almost as surprised as she is. He nods profusely, smiling, feeling very smug*

**Man Miguel** Sí, I remember. I always remember. We go now, eh?

**Woman Lorna** Not yet. I want to ask you something first. (*Pause*) If you've been thinking of me for twenty-five years every time you've made love, how come you didn't recognize me when I first arrived?

**Man Miguel** I know you straightway. First day arrived I know you woman of dreams.

**Woman Lorna** Then why didn't you say something?

*At this point Woman Regietta sneaks out of the hotel and looks on*

**Man Miguel** I 'fraid, you know? You no say nothing either. Me think you no remember me so I er... how you say — pretend? Yeah, pretend. So I pretend no know you.

**Woman Lorna** You know I can almost believe that.

*Woman Regietta crosses the terrace stealthily*

**Man Miguel** 'Tis true. Please, we go now. You make way up hill, down hill, I see you bottom eh? Sí.

*Woman Lorna goes off L in the direction of the secret place*

*Man Miguel turns and jumps as he sees Woman Regietta standing behind him. He starts shouting*

Aahh! Why you do that! You always do that! You frighten shit, you know?

**Woman Regietta** (*shouting*) Where you go?

**Man Miguel** Where you think I go? I go get frozen water. We have no ice for drink. I go to town. Be one hour maybe.

**Woman Regietta** I bet you go to town. You always go to town. You no gentle no more.

**Man Miguel** How you know? You always too hot to know.

**Woman Regietta** Where she go?

**Man Miguel** Who?
**Woman Regietta** English woman.
**Man Miguel** I no know. Maybe she go to beach. Maybe she go to shops.
**Woman Regietta** Or maybe she go to town with you, eh? (*She gyrates the lower part of her body*) Maybe you go to town together, you know.
**Man Miguel** Who are you, my wife?
**Woman Regietta** Sí!
**Man Miguel** (*determined*) You are no wife! I have no wife! Where is paper to say wife?
**Woman Regietta** You are father of my children.
**Man Miguel** Where is paper to say father?
**Woman Regietta** No need paper. Look at children face. They all ugly like you.
**Man Miguel** You are so beautiful?
**Woman Regietta** You think so once.
**Man Miguel** Once you were.
**Woman Regietta** You never say I beautiful.
**Man Miguel** What good it do? You no make love no more.
**Woman Regietta** (*slight pause*) Where you go? Tell truth.
**Man Miguel** Truth? What is truth? Truth is what everyone want to hear. Truth is what I tell.
**Woman Regietta** So ...you go get ice?
**Man Miguel** On way back get ice.
**Woman Regietta** (*shouting*) Where you go first?
**Man Miguel** On boat.
**Woman Regietta** You meet with her. You take her to secret place?
**Man Miguel** She no very happy.
**Woman Regietta** (*screaming*) I no very happy. I bloody furious.
**Man Miguel** Please. I pass. I need pack lunch.

*He moves to pass her but each time he attempts to Woman Regietta moves to block him*

**Woman Regietta** No!
**Man Miguel** I go get lunch for——
**Woman Regietta** No!
**Man Miguel** OK. I no have pack lunch. I go anyway, eh?

*He turns and is about to go off L when Woman Regietta calls after him*

**Woman Regietta** Miguel?

*He ignores her. She calls again*

Miguel!

*He stops and turns to look at her*

Maybe if you no go ... (*She sits at centre table* ) Maybe if baby sleep tonight.

*She attempts to put one leg on the table but can't do it without using her hands*

Maybe we make love, eh?
**Man Miguel** (*smiling as he moves a little nearer her* ) Maybe I rather go get frozen water, you know.

*He turns and leaves immediately*

*She stands and spits in his direction. After a moment she begins to clear the tables starting with the one* DR. *She finds Miguel's torn photograph. After looking at it she puts it in a safe place—down her chest. She crosses to clear the table far left*

*While Woman Regietta is doing this Dougie appears from behind the hotel still carrying the camera. He has seen Man Miguel exit and is looking off in that direction*

*Woman Regietta senses him there*

**Woman Regietta** Señor Dougie. Why you no go to Caves of Drach?
**Dougie** I missed the bus.
**Woman Regietta** Bus always late. Bus never go early.
**Dougie** Where's Miguel off to?
**Woman Regietta** He no tell. Regietta always have to guess, you know?

*Dougie puts the camera down on the table* DR. *As he does so he sees Woman Lorna's bag which she has left on one of the chairs*

**Dougie** Have you seen my wife?
**Woman Regietta** Sure.
**Dougie** (*picking up the bag and holding it up for Woman Regietta to see*)
Where is she?
**Woman Regietta** (*moving to centre table*) You guess. (*Pause*) Just like
before, eh señor Dougie? (*Tentatively*) You remember before?

*She very quickly yanks the band which holds her hair back. She shakes*
*her head and this sends her black hair cascading over her shoulders*

Many year ago—
**Dougie** Yes—of course ... yes.
**Woman Regietta** Ah, you prefer to forget, eh? I understand.
(*Slight pause*) I was very hurt, you know?
**Dougie** Hurt?
**Woman Regietta** Just like you.
**Dougie** (*slight pause*) I did it for spite.
**Woman Regietta** Just like me.
**Dougie** Didn't do either of us any good, did it?
**Woman Regietta** Oh no, no, no. (*She goes to him*) For me I felt very nice
for many days.

*Dougie is very flattered. He smiles as he moves towards Woman Regietta*

**Dougie** Thanks. (*He suddenly turns away*) I felt rotten for years. (*He*
*realises how that might have sounded*) Oh, I didn't mean—
**Woman Regietta** No, no señor. I know. Regietta woman. She understand. (*Slight pause*)

*Embarassed now, he looks away from her. Suddenly she is beside him.*
*Her two hands on his left shoulder*

You very special man señor Dougie. Señora Lorna very lucky woman.
**Dougie** I don't think she'd agree.
**Woman Regietta** (*slight pause*) You know I name first son for you.
**Dougie** (*smiling, pleased for a second as he realises the implication*)
What?
**Woman Regietta** No worry, señor—he no born till nineteen-seventy.
Four year after you leave, you know? S'OK.

Four year after you leave, you know? S'OK.

**Dougie** (*very flattered now* ) Oh... so you named your son after me then?

**Woman Regietta** Sí. Señor Douglas Rameris Travola. He very handsome boy. He work very hard in bar in Alcudia. He hope one day to have own place. (*Slight pause* ) He favourite. He favourite 'cause of you.

**Dougie** Now you're embarrassing me.

**Woman Regietta** I sorry. I no wish do that. (*She goes back to centre table. A pause* ) You never tell señora Lorna what happened between us?

**Dougie** No. (*Slight pause* ) Did you tell Miguel?

**Woman Regietta** Never. Once I tell him take weight on elbow, you know? (*She taps her elbow* ) But he never. Not no in thirty year he do like you.

*They both laugh awkwardly*

**Dougie** I knew all this would happen you know.

*Woman Regietta looks at him. She doesn't understand what he means*

Lorna and Miguel. I think that's why I brought her back. It's all a bit of a mess, really. The thing is, she's been holding a torch for him ever since we first came here.

**Woman Regietta** Torch? How torch?

**Dougie** (*explaining* ) She's liked him for a very long time. I don't know what I'm hoping for ... but I don't want to lose her. I'm thinking maybe the only way I can keep her is to let her go.

**Woman Regietta** How you do that? How you keep her and let her go, I no understand.

**Dougie** (*moving a chair slightly away from centre table and sitting on it*) I mean it hasn't been a terrible marriage. She can be a lot of fun when she wants to. And she was marvellous with the kids.

**Woman Regietta** Miguel he no good father. He no bad but he no good, you know? He like to make baby, but he no like be father. (*She moves behind him and running her two hands down his chest leaves them there*) You like to make baby señor?

**Dougie** Well... um... I —

**Woman Regietta** If still hurt, maybe hurt go way.

**Dougie** I'm very flattered, really I am but—

**Woman Regietta** But Regietta too fat now, eh?

**Dougie**  No, no, no, I like fat women — I do, really.
**Woman Regietta**  If close eyes I maybe like I was for you.
**Dougie**  (*putting his finger inside the rim of his collar*) I don't know what
to say here.
**Woman Regietta**  You hot?

*He nods*

I go get drink — make cool. I know we have plenty ice. You stay. You
no go way.

*Dougie smiles and nods ever so slightly*

*Woman Regietta goes into the hotel*

*A second or two later, Girl Regietta appears from* L. *She walks onto the
terrace and is obviously upset. She sees the back of Dougie at the table
and runs across the terrace hoping that he doesn't hear her, but he does*

*He calls to her immediately and she stops*

**Dougie**  Regietta? What is it? What's the matter?

*She doesn't turn to face him but he can tell she is upset*

*He goes to her*

What's happened?  Someone's upset you?

*She can't answer him*

Come and sit down.

*She doesn't really want to but he physically leads her to sit at the
centre table*

Come on, I'm sure it's not as bad as all that.

*Before she has the chance to answer Woman Regietta returns from the hotel carrying a tray on which are a bottle of wine and two drinks*

**Woman Regietta** Señor Dougie, you remember how upset I was all those
years ago?
**Dougie** I remember.

*Lighting changes so that Dougie and Girl Regietta are in spot*

**Woman Regietta** You were very nice to me. I cry so much you give me—
how you say?
**Dougie** Handkerchief?

*He offers a handkerchief to Girl Regietta. She takes it*

**Woman Regietta** I blow nose.

*Girl Regietta blows her nose and immediately offers the hanky back but
Dougie declines*

But you no want to take back. I wash it, I keep in drawer in hotel
bedroom. Silly, eh?

*Dougie smiles at Woman Regietta*

Then I remember you tell to go to room.

*Dougie slips his hand under Girl Regietta's arm and helps her to her feet*

*She gets up from the table and goes off into the hotel. Dougie follows her*

I know you follow.

*As Dougie is about opposite Woman Regietta she stops him by putting her
hand on his shoulder*

*Revert back to previous lighting*

**Woman Regietta** You no tell to go to room today?

*There is a pause before Dougie smiles and shakes his head*

**Dougie** We don't want each other today anymore than we did twenty-five
years ago. Let's drown our sorrows instead, shall we?

*Woman Regietta smiles at him and nods. She picks up the tray with the two
glasses and bottle of wine and takes them to the centre table*

**Woman Regietta** If you had one wish, señor—what you wish?
**Dougie** (*slight pause* ) Oh I just want Lorna back.
**Woman Regietta** (*pouring* ) Drink. Make wish. Sometimes come true.
**Dougie** You think?
**Woman Regietta** Sure. (*She hands him a glass of wine* )

*They tap each other's glass then drink together*

**Dougie** What did you wish?
**Woman Regietta** I tell, maybe not happen.
**Dougie** I wish there was something we could do. To change things. Bring
things to a head. Make everything right again.
**Woman Regietta** Have more drink. Make more wishes, eh?
**Dougie** (*inspired* ) Hey, wait a minute. (*He smiles* ) Maybe there is
something we can do.
**Woman Regietta** Tell.
**Dougie** And who knows, we might even get Miguel back on the straight
and narrow.
**Woman Regietta** Share with me.
**Dougie** (*laughing* ) I think I've got an idea. (*Convinced* ) Yes I have. And
if you come along with me we might just pull it off.
**Woman Regietta** Pull it off?
**Dougie** A toast! To you and me, Lorna and Miguel and a couple of Spanish
lies.

*A bar or two of aggressive Spanish music*

*Black-out*

# ACT II

## SCENE 1

*Later the same evening*

*Throughout the following scene Dougie is drunk to everyone except in his replies to Girl Lorna who is wearing a bandage on one leg and sitting at the same table on the opposite side of Dougie*

*The candles are now lit on each of the small tables. People have eaten and are now, and have been for some time, drinking heavily. The cabaret is about to begin. The two Miguels introduce it, as the act is the same and hasn't changed in twenty-five years*

**Man Miguel**  Please, ladies and gentlemen.
**Boy Miguel**  As you know, it is tradition in our country to dance —
**Man Miguel**  For you after you have —
**Boy Miguel**  Enjoyed —
**Man Miguel**  Your —
**Boy Miguel**  Meal.
**Man Miguel**  It is my —
**Boy Miguel**  Pleasure now —
**Man Miguel**  To introduce our dancer for the evening.
**Boy Miguel**  I'm sure she is no stranger to you—
**Man Miguel**  As she is a very familiar person, if you know what I mean.
**Boy Miguel**  Please — I give to you—
**Man Miguel**  Señorita —
**Boy Miguel**  Regietta!

*Spanish music is heard and Girl Regietta appears from the hotel and takes up her position on the terrace. She is wearing a brilliant red Spanish dress and has a red rose between her teeth*

*More music is heard and she is followed by Woman Regietta*

*She is wearing an identical dress but it is ill-fitting because of all the weight she has put on over the years. No other change has been made and the red rose between the teeth has remained*

*They do the dance simultaneously. Girl Regietta is very good at it but Woman Regietta has become bored over the years and simply goes through the motions with very little or no effort whatsoever*

*During the dance Girl Regietta attempts to get Dougie onto the floor to join her, but he refuses. Woman Regietta invites him and he jumps at the opportunity*

*The dance finishes with Girl Regietta at the hotel doorway. She disppears into the hotel the minute she finishes*

*Woman Regietta is in the middle of the dance area with her foot resting on Dougie's chest. He is flat out on his back. Applause*

*Woman Regietta helps Dougie to his feet. He sits back at the table with Woman Lorna*

*Woman Regietta smiles at Dougie and throws him a very passionate kiss and goes into the hotel*

*Man Miguel is in line of this and turns to see it was meant for Dougie who is vigorously returning the gesture*

**Woman Lorna**  All right, all right—there's no need to go overboard.
**Dougie**  Listen to you—you sound quite jealous.
**Woman Lorna**  I just don't like you making a fool of yourself, that's all.
**Dougie**  And it wouldn't do for the two of us to do that, would it?
**Man Miguel**  (*to Dougie* ) More drinks, señor?
**Dougie**  Why not. (*He drinks up the remaining lager in his glass and hands it to Man Miguel* ) I'll have the same again. What about you, Lorna? Can Miguel get you something? Or has he given you enough? (*To Man Miguel* ) I'll tell you what, Miguel— why don't you fix her one of your special cocktails. Something with a real bang in it. She could do with loosening up.
**Woman Lorna**  (*to Dougie* ) Just because I didn't make a fool of myself dancing it doesn't mean that I'm not having a good time!

*Dougie makes a face at Man Miguel*

I'll have a Harvey Wallbanger!
**Man Miguel** Sí.

*He goes off into the hotel to prepare drinks*

*Boy Miguel remains outside not too far away from Girl Lorna*

**Girl Lorna** If I didn't know better I'd say you were pouting.
**Woman Lorna** What the hell have I got to pout about?
**Dougie** (*to Woman Lorna* ) You tell *me* ! (*To Girl Lorna* ) You know exactly what the matter is.
**Girl Lorna** I only said I might meet you off the boat.
**Dougie** (*to Girl Lorna* ) That's not what I'm on about.
**Woman Lorna** There isn't anything wrong with me.
**Dougie** (*to Woman Lorna* ) Then why are you so miserable?
**Girl Lorna** It's probably my leg. You should have seen the blisters.
**Dougie** (*to Girl Lorna* ) Well if you hadn't insisted on me going off for the day on my own, I might have.
**Woman Lorna** I'm sorry I didn't come with you now.
**Girl Lorna** It was all all right. Miguel looked after me. It was him who took me to the hospital.
**Boy Miguel** Sí, señor. I take good care. I watch, no harm, you know.
**Girl Lorna** There. Now I hope you're going to drop all this nonsense and start to enjoy yourself.
**Dougie** (*to Woman Lorna* ) But if you don't, it makes no difference because I'm going to let my hair down any way.
**Woman Lorna** Big deal — you haven't got that much.
**Dougie** Look, shall we call a truce?
**Girl Lorna** I will —
**Woman Lorna** If you will.
**Girl Lorna** (*to Dougie* ) So what do you say?
**Dougie** (*to Girl Lorna* ) I haven't got much choice.
**Girl Lorna** (*to Dougie* ) Do you mind if I dance with Miguel?

*Dougie is about to interject*

Only I know it's not your scene.

*Girl Lorna doesn't wait for an answer.* She *and Boy Miguel get up and dance*

*After watching Girl Lorna and Boy Miguel dance for a second or two, Dougie turns to Woman Lorna*

**Dougie** I didn't want to say this tonight but I suppose this is as good a time as any. ( *He gets up and moves* DR) It's over. Finished.

**Woman Lorna** What is ?

**Dougie** I want a divorce.

**Woman Lorna** You do?

**Dougie** (*moving back towards her slightly* ) Now I don't want it to turn out all ugly and horrible.

**Woman Lorna** What are you talking about?

**Dougie** (*slight pause* ) There's someone else, Lorna ... and they've come between us for long enough now.

**Woman Lorna** No!

**Dougie** Yes! It's time to come clean, and be honest with each other. No more lies, you know?

**Woman Lorna** ( *slight pause; gettting up and moving* DL ) I bet you've been talking to your Regietta, haven't you?

**Dougie** Yes, of course I have. As a matter of fact we've discussed it in detail.

**Woman Lorna** I could deny everything, but if you've known from the start, I don't see the point.

**Dougie** I'm sorry I'm not with you.

**Woman Lorna** Me and Miguel. For what it's worth it doesn't mean anything anymore. It took a long time to get him out of my system but I have, finally. Ironic, isn't it? The minute I get everything into perspective I get caught.

**Dougie** Lorna, what are you talking about?

**Woman Lorna** I did hope we could get on with our lives now ... build the marriage, but I can see by your reaction it's not on.

**Dougie** Are you telling me, you and Miguel have been having a fling?

**Woman Lorna** It's all over now. Not that it was ever much of a fling for him in the first place. (*It finally dawns on her* ) You mean you didn't know?

**Dougie** I'm afraid not, no.

**Woman Lorna** But ... what did you mean when you said ...

**Dougie**  When I said there was someone else I didn't mean with you. I
  meant with me.
**Woman Lorna** (*slight pause* ) Shit!

*Woman Regietta comes out with a tray and two drinks — a Harvey
Wallbanger and pint of lager. She puts the tray down at Dougie's table*

**Woman Regietta**  Everything OK for you?
**Dougie**  Everything is wonderful. (*He puts his arm around Woman
  Regietta's shoulders* ) I've just told Lorna about us.
**Woman Lorna**  (*screaming* ) Us!!
**Woman Regietta**  You tell her you love me?
**Dougie**  I've just asked for a divorce, yes.
**Woman Lorna**  (*to Dougie* )You're not serious?
**Woman Regietta**  OK to tell Miguel now, eh?
**Dougie**  Why not?

*Woman Regietta puts her arms around Dougie and gives him a huge kiss
on each cheek*

**Woman Regietta** (*running off into the hotel* ) Hey, Miguel, guess what ...
  I got something to tell you.

*She laughs as she disappears inside*

*Dougie watches her go, then turns to Woman Lorna who is still looking
on in total disbelief*

**Dougie**  (*turning to face Woman Lorna* ) Isn't she wonderful?
**Woman Lorna** (*going towards him but standing left of the table of drinks*)
  You've flipped, haven't you?
**Dougie**  I'm absolutely smitten with her.
**Woman Lorna** (*sitting at the table* )  You can't be yourself — you must
  have had too much sun.
**Dougie**  You're right, I'm not myself. I'm happier now than I've ever
  been.
**Woman Lorna**  Look, we've got plenty of insurance—let me phone a
  doctor—there's got to be something wrong with your head.
**Dougie**  Why? There was nothing wrong with yours.

**Woman Lorna** It's ...( *lost for words* ) ... outrageous.
**Dougie** Why is it anymore outrageous for me than it is for you?
**Woman Lorna** (*shouting at him*) You've only got to look at her for God's sake.
**Dougie** OK she's no beauty ... ( *He  sits at the table* ) I'll tell you what though — she's got lovely skin.

*Woman Lorna takes this remark very personally. Dougie turns his head away from her for her not to see him smile*

**Woman Lorna** ( *slight pause* ) She's hardly your type.
**Dougie** Oh, so you know my type now, do you?
**Woman Lorna** I thought I knew, yes.
**Dougie** And I thought I knew a lot of things.
**Woman Lorna** (*slight pause;looking at Dougie very hard then starts to laugh suspiciously*) It's a joke, isn't it? You can't really have fallen for someone like that.
**Dougie** Why not? She's a very sincere and genuine person. I've already booked her a seat on the plane home.
**Woman Lorna** (*outraged* ) You're taking her home?
**Dougie** Well I didn't plan on settling down and opening a bar here.
**Woman Lorna** (*brief pause* ) What about the baby?
**Dougie** Oh she'll be bringing him with her, obviously.
**Woman Lorna** Oh, of course, yes ... obviously.
**Dougie** Didn't have to book a ticket for him though — kids travel free under two.

*A pause. Dougie takes a drink*

*Woman Lorna's brain is working overtime*

*Suddenly Dougie turns to Girl Lorna who is still dancing on Dougie's right with Boy Miguel*

**Dougie** ( *to Girl Lorna* ) Enjoying your honeymoon?
**Girl Lorna** One more dance and I'll sit back down.
**Dougie** Leg all right now is it?

*She quickly looks down at her bandaged leg which she has completely*

*forgotten about, then looks to Boy Miguel, then back over to Dougie. They
change from doing their original dance into something much slower*

**Woman Lorna** ( *to Dougie* ) Where will they live?
**Dougie** ( *turning back to Woman Lorna* ) Well with me of course.
**Woman Lorna** And where will *you* live?
**Dougie** Ah well that sort of depends on you.
**Woman Lorna** Me?
**Dougie** It's a bit soon to be discussing this sort of thing but I've already
given it some thought. The way I see it is this ... either you can stay in
the house and buy me out—
**Woman Lorna** (*standing as she shouts* ) How the hell can I buy you out
when I haven't got any money?
**Dougie** Maybe Miguel will help you out. If not, maybe now's the time to
start thinking about a job.
**Woman Lorna** (*not believing her ears* ) What!
**Dougie** You don't really expect me to carry on supporting you, do you?

*Woman Lorna is stunned*

Anyway, as I was saying—either you can stay in the house and buy *me*
out or I'll buy *you* out. It's your decision.
**Woman Lorna** (*moving* DL ) Some bloody decision.
**Dougie** (*picking up his lager and toasting her*) Isn't life a bitch. (*He takes
a mouthful*)

*Slight pause. She is devastated*

**Woman Lorna** What will the children think?
**Dougie** (*getting up and moving* DC ) Well she's told a few of them already
and apparently they're delighted.
**Woman Lorna** (*shouting* ) I meant our bloody kids!
**Dougie** To be honest I'm not really bothered. I know once they take one
look at Regietta they'll fall in love with her just like I did.

*At this point Girl Lorna and Boy Miguel stop dancing and come to sit on
the steps of the hotel* DR. *They talk very intimately throughout the following
scene*

**Woman Lorna** (*slight pause* ) Why am I finding all this difficult to
   believe?
**Dougie** Because it's the last thing you expected. You were so engrossed
   in your own little affair you were probably blind to mine.
**Woman Lorna** But ... you and Regietta.
**Dougie** It isn't so difficult to believe. I suppose it's all right to say now,
   you know but ... well we had a bit of a thing going when we first came
   here.
**Woman Lorna** In sixty-six?
**Dougie** Yeah. Fancy all those feelings rushing back after all those years.
**Woman Lorna** (*another bombshell; hitting Dougie on the shoulders* )
   Are you telling me you went with her on our honeymoon?
**Dougie** That's right. Awful isn't it? I must admit though I didn't feel bad
   about it at the time because I was convinced there was something going
   on with you and Miguel.

*At this point Man Miguel is heard laughing from inside the hotel*

*Woman Lorna and Dougie hear it immediately. The laughing gets louder
and hysterical*

*Eventually Man Miguel appears in the doorway of the hotel and is
almost helpless with laughter. He staggers over to the table* R. *He tries
to speak but every time he becomes more hysterical. After several
attempts he eventually manages to get something out — but still he
cannot contain his laughter*

**Man Miguel** (*laughing* ) Señor ... señor, Regietta ... she say very funny
thing, you know? I share with you? I tell what she say?

*He is still laughing. Dougie has joined in with him now and nods*

She say ... (*He can't control himself* )

*Woman Regietta comes to stand outside the doorway of the hotel. She
looks over at Man Miguel*

*Eventually Man Miguel squeezes out his line*

She say you love her and she go live with you in England. (*He launches into another fit of hysteria* )

*Dougie laughs with him before chipping in his line*

**Dougie**  It's true. I do... and she is.

*Man Miguel continues laughing for a few seconds but stops immediately when the words sink in*

**Man Miguel**  Beg pardon, señor?
**Dougie**  I think the world of her. (*He turns to face Woman Lorna* )And she loves me too.

*Woman Lorna storms off* L

**Man Miguel**  No, no — you no like Regietta.
**Dougie**  (*watching Woman Lorna as she goes* ) Why not?
**Man Miguel**  She ... (*He is lost for words. He mimes her size and shape*) You already have beautiful wife.
**Dougie**  (*turning to Man Miguel* ) So do you.
**Man Miguel**  (*still insisting* ) I have no wife.
**Dougie**  Good. For a minute there I thought we were going to have problems.
**Man Miguel**  Problems, señor?
**Dougie**  She's been here a long time, Miguel. It's not going to be easy to let her go.

*Woman Regietta comes over to join them*

**Woman Regietta**  Good help hard to find. Better start look soon, eh? I already move out of room. I sleep in small room on third floor.
**Man Miguel**  (*to Woman Regietta* ) You sure this you want?
**Woman Regietta**  What here to keep me?
**Man Miguel**  (*slight pause* ) OK — no problem. You go what day — Friday, eh?

*Girl Regietta calls to Boy Miguel from inside the hotel*

**Girl Regietta**(*off* ) Miguel, I busy in kitchen. You come take supper to father.

*Boy Miguel whispers something to Girl Lorna and then goes inside the hotel*

*After Boy Miguel has disappeared, Girl Lorna sneaks off around the back of the hotel*

**Woman Regietta** You pay me what you owe, Miguel?

**Man Miguel** (*not wanting to talk money in front of Dougie, he takes her by the elbow and leads her* DR ) What I owe? I no owe nothing.

**Woman Regietta** You owe wages. You no pay for thirty year.

*Dougie takes his lager and sits at table* L

**Man Miguel** (*taking a wad of notes out of his back pocket* ) How much I owe? You tell how much I owe? (*He licks his thumb and starts to count out a couple of notes* )

**Woman Regietta** One hundred thousand peseta.

**Man Miguel** (*putting the money back immediately* ) You crazy woman, you know?

**Woman Regietta** You no pay me?

**Man Miguel** Miguel he no have that much money.

**Woman Regietta** You lie. I know where you keep.

**Man Miguel** I no pay. You big fat woman—I feed for long time. Regietta already have wages.

**Woman Regietta** OK — you no pay. (*She takes off her apron as she crosses in front of him. She puts the apron on the back of the chair* ) But Regietta she no work, you know?

**Man Miguel** How you mean no work?

**Woman Regietta** (*shouting* ) No work! I no cook, no clean, serve paella, make bed, I do nothing! Entiende?

**Man Miguel** S'OK with me. I run hotel before you come, you know?

**Woman Regietta** Huh! You run hotel with father before he go crazy. What you do? You bring him from attic to help now, eh? He frighten shit out of guest, you make no money, you starve, you die, who care. Regietta live in very nice... (*To Dougie* ) how you say?

**Dougie** Bungalow.

**Woman Regietta**  Very nice bungalow on side of mountain in England.
**Dougie**  (*correcting her* ) Ystrad.
**Woman Regietta**  Ystrad.
**Man Miguel**  You think I no do well with you no here?
**Woman Regietta**  Maybe. I no care no more. I guest now. I sit. (*She sits next to Dougie* ) Señor Dougie buy drink for me. You serve and be nice to me and maybe I leave tip, eh?
**Dougie**  I've got a drink, but what would you like?
**Woman Regietta**  Regietta would like maybe something long.
**Man Miguel**  Sí. And the longer the better.

*Woman Regietta turns sharply to him but he turns away waving his hand to dismiss her*

*He goes inside to get the drink*

**Woman Regietta**  (*excited* ) What you think, señor? Everything go to plan, eh?
**Dougie**  Well it was a real smack in the mouth for Lorna. I'm not sure how we're doing with Miguel though.
**Woman Regietta**  Ah he very worry man. He no show, but he very worry man.
**Dougie**  Good. And we've certainly given Lorna something to think about.
**Woman Regietta**  What we do next, señor? I start to enjoy, you know?
**Dougie**  Well I think I'd better find somewhere to sleep tonight. (*He takes a mouthful of lager* )
**Woman Regietta**  I thought maybe we sleep together.
**Dougie**  (*almost choking* ) But that might spoil everything,
**Woman Regietta**  I no mean same bed. Same room. Make think same bed.
**Dougie**  (*laughing* ) You're latching on to this very well, aren't you? OK, come on. Come and give me a hand to move my things out of my room.

*They both get up and go towards the hotel. As they are about to enter Man Miguel comes out with Woman Regietta's long drink*

*Dougie walks past him and into the hotel*

*Woman Regietta remains to have a quick word*

**Woman Regietta** (*to Man Miguel*) You put on table. I go help put señor
Dougie move things to new room.
**Man Miguel** What new room?
**Woman Regietta** (*smiling*) My new room.

*Woman Regietta laughs hysterically as she exits into the hotel*

*As Man Miguel puts her drink down on the table, Woman Lorna comes
back onto the terrace*

*Man Miguel sees her*

*Girl Lorna reappears from behind the hotel. She comes to sit on right
side of centre table*

**Man Miguel** Ah señora — you return.

*Woman Lorna smiles a little uncomfortably*

**Man Miguel** You go for walk, eh?
**Woman Lorna** Where have they gone?
**Man Miguel** They go to room. They move things. They have own room
now.

*This news bothers Woman Lorna*

**Woman Lorna** How can Regietta do this?
**Man Miguel** I tell you — she very creep up woman.
**Woman Lorna** What am I going to do?
**Man Miguel** Tonight we talk. I come to room and after we talk.
**Woman Lorna** After what?
**Man Miguel** After we make love of course.

*Woman Lorna doesn't answer. He turns to go and she calls him*

**Woman Lorna** Miguel?
**Man Miguel** Sí?
**Woman Lorna** (*very sweetly*) Piss off?
**Man Miguel** (*laughing*) Of course. You know where is. You no need ask.

*He exits into the hotel*

*Woman Lorna's reaction to his answer is to laugh, but it's a very ironic and sarcastic laugh. She comes to sit at the same table as Girl Lorna. She sits still, laughing. She throws her head back as she becomes more hysterical. But as she brings her head forward her laughter turns to crying*

*Girl Lorna looks at her*

**Girl Lorna**  Oh dear ... Miguel was a disaster, then?
**Woman Lorna**  Dougie was right. Twenty-five years in this heat has wrinkled everything. (*Slight pause* ) I don't know what's going to happen to me. Dougie's talking about buying me out. Can you imagine me living anywhere else?
**Girl Lorna**  No.
**Woman Lorna**  Thank God for that.
**Girl Lorna**  I can see you helping out here though.
**Woman Lorna**  What!
**Girl Lorna**  Any minute now he's going to come and ask you.

*Man Miguel comes to stand in the hotel doorway*

**Man Miguel**  Señora Lorna?
**Woman Lorna**  What did I tell you.
**Man Miguel**  I have tiny, tiny problem.
**Woman Lorna**  I know you have, Miguel.
**Man Miguel**  You do favour for me, eh?
**Woman Lorna**  (*shaking her head* ) I've already done one favour too many for you.
**Man Miguel**  Please?
**Woman Lorna**  What is it?
**Man Miguel**  (*trying to take her hand* ) Come, I tell inside.
**Woman Lorna**  (*snatching it back* ) No, you tell me out here.
**Man Miguel**  You come to kitchen—
**Woman Lorna**  (*standing* ) I'm not cooking anything.
**Man Miguel**  No, no, Miguel cook.
**Woman Lorna**  So what do you want then?
**Man Miguel**  (*slight pause* ) You come kill cockroach for me, eh?

Regietta, she would do with big shoe, you know? Miguel no like —
always make feel sick. You have big foot like Regietta — I only size
thirty-eight, you know?

**Woman Lorna** Well, if you didn't shatter all my illusions this afternoon
Miguel, you've shattered them now. Fancy you being afraid of a little
thing like that.

**Man Miguel** Please, you do for me?

**Woman Lorna** (*taking off her shoe* ) Where is it?

**Man Miguel** On floor in kitchen.

*Woman Lorna walks past him and goes into the hotel*

*After a few seconds we can hear the shoe being slammed onto the floor
several times*

*After a few seconds Woman Lorna comes back out onto the terrace*

**Man Miguel** You kill dead?

**Woman Lorna** (*going to him* ) It's the flattest cockroach I've ever seen.
Look !

*She opens her fist and pretends to have it in her palm. Man Miguel doesn't
realize she is playing a joke on him and almost jumps out of his skin. She
chases him with it around the terrace — possibly to the music of the
William Tell Overture*

*The lights fade*

*Black-out*

SCENE 2

*Lights come up and it's about ten in the morning. One or two people
are still finishing breakfast. Girl Lorna is sitting at a table. She has a
well packed beach-bag. Woman Lorna, smoking, sits alone at a table
not too far away, in a chair which she has pulled away slightly from
one of the tables. Her shoes are on the floor beside her and she is now
wearing the apron Woman Regietta left over the chair in the previous
scene. She sits and looks zombie-like. Woman Regietta sits at another
table. She is holding her young baby in her arms*

*After a few seconds, Boy Miguel comes out of the hotel carrying a tray.*
*A couple get up and wave to him as they leave. After smiling at Girl*
*Lorna he goes straight to their table to pick up the money which they*
*have left for him. He starts to clear things away. He speaks to Girl*
*Lorna who is at the next table*

**Boy Miguel**  Where you go today?
**Girl Lorna**  We're having a day on the beach.
**Boy Miguel**   To work on tan, eh?
**Girl Lorna**  There'll be nothing else to do. I'll cover myself with oil and
   burn to a crisp — and Dougie'll find a nice comfortable spot in the shade
   and fall asleep. (*Sarcastically* ) I'm really looking forward to it.
**Boy Miguel**  Only two more day and you go home.
**Girl Lorna**  Two days, one night. I'm dreading it. I don't want to go home,
   Miguel.
**Boy Miguel**  (*secretively* ) You, er ... enjoy swim last night?

*Girl Lorna smiles and nods*

   One more night left. We do again, eh?
**Girl Lorna**  Oh yes. Just as soon as Dougie hits the pillow.
**Boy Miguel**   Where is señor Dougie now?
**Girl Lorna**  He's just popped back to the room. I forgot to pack his
   sunglasses. (*She rolls her eyes* )

*A string of Spanish from Girl Regietta is heard coming from the*
*hotel*

   I think I'd better go and chivvy him up.

*She gets up and goes in the direction of the hotel, leaving her beach-bag*
*on the floor at the table*

**Boy Miguel**  You have good time, eh?

   *Girl Lorna makes a face and goes inside the hotel*

   *Another couple leave their table and walk off the terrace*

*BoyMiguel has now cleared the table he was working on and goes back
inside the hotel*

*This leaves Woman Lorna and Woman Regietta alone on stage. After a
reasonable pause Woman Regietta snaps her fingers several times. She
fails to get Woman Lorna's attention. She reverts to tapping on the
table. This works as Woman Lorna looks over at her*

**Woman Regietta** I would like something to drink.
**Woman Lorna** *(after looking over her shoulder and realising she is
talking to her )* Go and get it then.
**Woman Regietta** You no serve me?
**Woman Lorna** *(firmly )* I don't work here! I'm helping out, that's all.
**Woman Regietta** *(getting up and going to her )* I sorry for you, señora.
You lose good man, you know? Me? I lose fat pig. *(Slight pause )* So—
you love señor Miguel now, eh?
**Woman Lorna** *(emphatically )* No! God no. I thought I could—but no.
Definitely, definitely no!
**Woman Regietta** *(smiling to herself, obviously very pleased to hear this.
Slight pause. )* Why you change mind, señora?

*Woman Lorna can't find the words to answer her. She shrugs her
shoulders and shakes her head*

He take you to secret place yesterday...

*Woman Lorna looks at her, uncomfortable in the knowledge that Woman
Regietta is aware the place exists*

Aahhh—he disappoint you, eh?

*She doesn't answer*

I say to him for long time now, "You use too much—you wear away, you
know?" *(A pause )* Where he tell he take today?
**Woman Lorna** Nowhere.
**Woman Regietta** He no ask to go get fish?
**Woman Lorna** Oh he asked me, yes.
**Woman Regietta** You refuse?

**Woman Lorna**  In so many words.
**Woman Regietta**  What you say?
**Woman Lorna**  Actually I answered him in sign language.

*Dougie, wearing sunglasses, and Girl Lorna come out of the hotel*

**Girl Lorna**  Come on, hurry up. Let's get a sunbed before they all go.

*She picks up her beach-bag and exits. Dougie follows immediately*

**Woman Regietta**  (*confirming* ) But you do work for him, eh?

*She sits at Woman Lorna's table*

**Woman Lorna**  I'm helping out that's all.
**Woman Regietta**  He promise to pay?
**Woman Lorna**  Oh yes.
**Woman Regietta**  You never get. Take tip — get wage now. He no
backdate, you know?

*Dougie, without sunglasses, comes back on to the terrace and goes over
to Woman Regietta and Woman Lorna*

**Dougie**  (*to Woman Regietta* ) Aahh —There you are. Oh, you've got
the baby. Can I hold him? ( *He sits at the table with the women either
side of him* )

*Woman Regietta hands him the baby*

**Dougie**  Good God! He's a spit of Miguel, isn't he? Look Lorna, look at
him.

*Woman Lorna turns her head — she's not in the least bit interested*

*A slight pause*

*Woman Regietta stands now behind Dougie*

Sleep all right last night?

**Woman Lorna** What do *you* think? (*Slight pause* ) I won't ask you the same.

**Woman Regietta** No, no, no, no. We no sleep. Stay wake most of night.

*She runs her hand around Dougie's neck. She and Dougie laugh. Woman Lorna can hardly contain her anger*

**Woman Lorna** Actually, I slept like a kitten myself.

**Dougie** Yes, we thought heard you purring most of the night.

**Woman Regietta** We stay in room above, you know?

**Woman Lorna** (*shouting* ) Are you saying I snore? Because you know very well I don't.

**Dougie** ( *putting his finger to his lips* ) Ssshh. ( *He points to the baby* )

*Woman Lorna turns away from him in her chair*

Perhaps it was Miguel then.

**Woman Lorna** ( *turning back towards him* ) Miguel wasn't in my room last night.

**Woman Regietta** Ooohhh ... we heard him knock you.

**Woman Lorna** Oh he knocked me—but I didn't let him in.

**Dougie** Things not working out between you?

**Woman Lorna** Well ... he's offered me a position in the kitchen.

**Dougie** You can't cook.

**Woman Lorna** I don't have to cook. I'm head cockroach killer. Can you believe he's afraid of them?

**Woman Regietta** Ah he no like creepy crawl. No spider, no cockroach, no lizard — nothing.

**Dougie** (*standing* ) Look, I've got to go. Oh, would you like to hold the baby, Lorna?

*Woman Lorna mouths "piss off ". Dougie turns to Woman Regietta*

She said she'll have him later.

*He hands the baby back to Woman Regietta who sits back down*

There you are. I want to make a couple of phone calls and I don't really want to use the telephone here. (*To Woman Regietta* ) Do you want to

come?
**Woman Regietta**  Better I put little one to bed, eh?
**Dougie**  OK, I'll only be about twenty minutes anyway.

*Dougie exits*

*Woman Lorna watches him go. She then looks at Woman Regietta*

**Woman Lorna**  ( *a slight pause; getting up and moving* DR ) I've made
a terrible fool of myself, haven't I?
**Woman Regietta**  Sí.
**Woman Lorna**  I don't know what to say to you, but for what it's worth
... I'm sorry.
**Woman Regietta** (*standing* ) Who you sorry for? Señor Dougie? Me
maybe? No need feel sorry for me. You live in very nice "bungalow" in
Ystrad. I know I very happy there. (*Slight pause* ) Maybe feel sorry for
self, eh? (*A pause* ) I tell you something Señora Lorna?

*They look at each other. Slight pause*

I tell secret to you — you promise no never tell Miguel?

*Woman Lorna nods and sits back down at the table*

Many years ago when very handsome he make love no problem. Now
'tis very hard for him 'cos always very soft. He want all time to light
oven but always match too damp, you know? He no like to fail but want
to try to prove always. But ... he no can cook no more. All remain, two
hungry people. (*Slight pause* ) Sad eh?

*They laugh together*

*After a moment or two Man Miguel steps out from inside the hotel*

**Man Miguel** (*seeing Woman Lorna's shoes at her side* ) Ah you rest feet.
You tired, eh?
**Woman Lorna**  Tired? I'm absolutely knackered.
**Man Miguel**  Tuesday very quiet. Wednesday busy night for us.
**Woman Lorna** (*putting on her shoes* ) Well I hope for your sake you've

found some help, Miguel, because I won't be able to do much for you tomorrow— I've got to pack and everything. (*She moves away* DL )
**Woman Regietta** I pack today. I all ready for tomorrow.

*Man Miguel hears this but decides to retort by speaking to Woman Lorna*

**Man Miguel** (*slight pause* ) You like to stay? You very good on tables.
**Woman Regietta** Good? Huh!
**Woman Lorna** She's right. You should have seen it out here, it was like a free for all. I didn't know what day it was.
**Man Miguel** You make look very easy.
**Woman Lorna** How would you know — you were tucked away in the kitchen. It was awful. I got everything wrong.
**Man Miguel** I had no complaints.
**Woman Lorna** No, because I had them all. I've never been so rushed in all my life. I'm surprised I didn't disappear up my backside. (*She gets up and demonstrates how busy it was* ) Right, what was it you said? One large beer, two small and a Coke—hang on a minute.(*To someone else*) I'll take your order for food now.(*She calls to a different couple* ) Thank you very much—hope you enjoyed it. (*To someone else* ) Sorry, what did you say? Yes, wait a sec. Forget the Coke — right. One Fanta Lemon instead.(*She shouts to another couple* ) No, we don't do curry and chips. (*To someone else* ) Well *somebody* ordered three Bacardi. (*To someone else* ) Try the calamari. (*To someone else* )No, there's no entertainment tonight. Paella for you, isn't it? (*To someone else* ) It's like elastic bands in batter, dear. Stuffed peppers and chilli? (*She shouts to someone else*) Hang on a minute — you haven't paid your bill. Who ordered the ice-cream special? Anybody got change of a five thousand? (*She screams*) Well it's not my fault — see the boss. (*To someone else* ) Yes, thank you very much.(*She shouts way over the top* ) No, you can't alter your friggin' order! Me—I'm the bloody cabaret! (*She ends up in frenzy and collapses back down in the chair. To Woman Regietta* ) I don't know how you did it, honest I don't.
**Woman Regietta** I do for long time. No problem for me now. No problem me now anyway. Tomorrow I fly to Ystrad. (*She sniffs the air; to the baby* ) Oh no, why you do again, eh? Always I change you make smell. (*To the others* ) S'cuse, eh?

*She exits into hotel*

**Woman Lorna** She's a very good mother.
**Man Miguel** She have plenty practice.

*Man Miguel comes to sit down at the table* L

**Woman Lorna** Practice doesn't always make perfect— otherwise you'd
be good at a lot of things.
**Man Miguel** (*slight pause*) You change, you know? Miguel he think you
no like him no more.
**Woman Lorna** Of course I like you ... it's just—
**Man Miguel** Why you no let in to room last night?
**Woman Lorna** You were knocking at the wrong door.
**Man Miguel** I was? (*He thinks about it for a moment*) No, no I know your
room. I knock at right door.
**Woman Lorna** (*going to sit at the table with him*) You don't get it, do
you? (*Slight pause*) I've had my chips with Dougie.
**Man Miguel** No, no my friend. You know what I think? I think you and
me maybe have had chips.
**Woman Lorna** (*slight pause*) I bet if you asked Regietta to stay she
would.
**Man Miguel** You like me to do that for me or for you?
**Woman Lorna** (*smiling*) You're no fool, are you? (*Slight pause*) Put it
this way, Miguel ... I think perhaps we owe it to each other.
**Man Miguel** (*slight pause*) I no can do, you know? I no never ask woman
for nothing ... but love.
**Woman Lorna** You mean sex.
**Man Miguel** Same thing, eh?
**Woman Lorna** Good God no. There's a huge difference between them.
**Man Miguel** You tell.
**Woman Lorna** Making love was something you did years ago success-
fully. Sex is what you tried to have yesterday and failed. You've lost the
art, Miguel. You were like me on those tables. You rushed it and got in
a hell of a mess. Making love with you used to be a three course meal.
Now it's just a ham sandwich. (*Slight pause*) Maybe it always *was* a
ham sandwich and I only thought it was *á la carte*. (*Slight pause*) No,
it's not that I don't like you anymore ... it's just that I've realised I'd
rather skip lunch.
**Man Miguel** (*moving up one chair to sit next to her*) When you last 'eat'

with señor Dougie?

**Woman Lorna** Oh, we've been on a diet for a long time.

**Man Miguel** You hungry now?

**Woman Lorna** Starving ... but I'm not eating out. (*Slight pause* ) If you will persuade Regietta to stay—when I get back home maybe I can cook a meal and ask Dougie round. Follow me?

**Man Miguel** What you cook ? Maybe you give Miguel recipe eh?

**Woman Lorna** You want *me* to tell you how to do it?

**Man Miguel** Sí.

**Woman Lorna** Right. (*She gets up and moves* c ) All you've got to do is put the roast in and cook it slow and I mean slow on a very low heat. Do you know what I mean?

**Man Miguel** (*joining her* ) I know what you mean.

*Dougie comes back on to the terrace. He sees the two of them talking and stays out of sight towards the back*

**Woman Lorna** The secret I always think is to heat the oven for a least half an hour first, you get me?

**Man Miguel** (*getting carried away* ) Sí, sí I get.

**Woman Lorna** Are you following me?

**Man Miguel** I follow señora.

**Woman Lorna** Then if you still find it tough—you stick it back in for a bit longer. But whatever you do, Miguel—for God sake don't cover it with foil. (*She laughs and suddenly becomes aware of Dougie* ) That was quick.

**Dougie** Changed my mind. I can always give them a call in the morning.

**Woman Lorna** How long have you been standing there?

**Dougie** Long enough to catch the cookery lesson. (*Slight pause* ) Can I have a 'San Miguel', Miguel? What about Lorna? Can Miguel get you a 'San Miguel'? And have a 'San Miguel' yourself, Miguel.

**Man Miguel** (*uncertain* ) How many 'San Miguel' you want Miguel get?

**Dougie** (*showing him two fingers* ) Two.

*Man Miguel gets the message now and scurries off*

*There is a slight pause*

**Dougie** Er... listen. (*He walks* DR ) You don't have to worry about when we get home.

**Woman Lorna** (*going to him*) She's not going back with you now?

**Dougie** Oh yes. It's just that I won't be taking her back to the house straightaway. I thought I'd ask my mother if she can stay there until we can sort things out.

**Woman Lorna** She probably will. She's never liked me.

**Dougie** You've never given her a chance.

*A pause*

**Woman Lorna** It still on then? You haven't had second thoughts or anything?

**Dougie** Oh no, no. It's the real thing.

*Woman Lorna doesn't quite know what to say next. Dougie moves towards her*

Thought about what you'll do?

**Woman Lorna** (*sarcastically*) Not yet. I've been having such a wonderful time I haven't had time to think about it.

**Dougie** I'm sorry it's not working out for you.

**Woman Lorna** I bet you are.

**Dougie** No, I am. You see I'm so happy it's making me feel guilty and I know I haven't got any reason to feel like that because I could so easily have been in your shoes.

**Woman Lorna** You'd look a bit funny in mine, don't you think?

*They both almost laugh. An awkward pause. Suddenly they both start to say something together*

**Woman Lorna** Sorry.

**Dougie** No, go on.

**Woman Lorna** (*slight pause*) I was going to say I was just going up to bed.

**Dougie** Yes. I was going to say that I was only going to have one drink and I'll be up behind you.

**Woman Lorna** You mean behind Regietta.

**Dougie** Yes, of course I do.

*Another pause*

**Woman Lorna** It's very awkward, isn't it?
**Dougie** How do you mean?
**Woman Lorna** You and Regietta. The room above. (*Slight pause* ) Still
— it's no more than I deserve, I suppose.
**Dougie** It bothers you then?
**Woman Lorna** (*slight pause* ) I've got to go. I'm sleeping on my feet.

*Woman Lorna is just about to walk into the hotel when Man Miguel
comes out of the hotel carrying a tray with two glasses of beer. He passes
her, then turns and calls after her*

**Man Miguel** Señora? Thank you for just now. Miguel sleep better
tonight, eh? Even though still very hot.

*Woman Lorna looks up at Dougie who thinks he might know for a brief
second what he is thanking her for. She is eager to put the record straight*

**Woman Lorna** (*almost blurting it out* ) I gave him some advice. We
talked, that's all.

*Dougie and Woman Lorna stare at each other. Dougie's face registers
nothing*

*Eventually Woman Lorna goes into the hotel*

*As soon as she does, Dougie sighs*

**Man Miguel** (*handing him a beer* ) One large beer, señor.
**Dougie** I don't know why I'm drinking with you. I *should* be smashing
it over your head.
**Man Miguel** Maybe we smash over each other's head, eh?
**Dougie** Why should we do that?
**Man Miguel** Regietta no know but I find hanky many year ago in drawer
in bedroom. 'Tis very nice hanky. It have name in corner. (*Slight pause*)
You know she name son for you?
**Dougie** I gave her that hanky because she saw you take off with Lorna on
your motorbike and she was upset.

**Man Miguel** I know you gave her more than a hanky.

**Dougie** I know you gave Lorna more than a lift.

**Man Miguel** S'OK. She no care for me no more, you know?

**Dougie** What? She's told you that?

**Man Miguel** Sure.

**Dougie** (*smiling*) So she wasn't just saying it.

**Man Miguel** Why she do that?

**Dougie** Let me get this absolutely right, Miguel. She actually came out and told you to your face that she doesn't care for you anymore?

*Man Miguel nods*

*A pause*

(*Smiling*) I know exactly why I'm drinking with you, Miguel.

**Man Miguel** You do?

**Dougie** We're celebrating.

**Man Miguel** We are?

**Dougie** It's taken a long time but I knew after twenty-five years you'd either make or break my marriage.

*Dougie puts his drink down on the table and runs off into the hotel calling for Woman Regietta*

**Man Miguel** (*under his breath*) English — they crazy people, you know.

*He goes into the hotel*

*Pavarotti singing 'Nessun Dorma' can be heard playing in the background*

*Man Miguel goes inside the hotel as Boy Miguel comes out*

*He is carrying a bottle of wine which he puts down on a table. He looks off left. He is obviously waiting for someone. He spots them coming*

*It is Dougie and Girl Lorna. They have obviously been out somewhere for the evening and are now on their way to their room.*

*As they walk onto the terrace Boy Miguel shows Dougie the bottle of wine obviously offering it to him. He shakes his hand to decline and mimes he is going straight up to bed as he is shattered*

*Dougie enters the hotel*

*Girl Lorna is about to go into the hotel but then turns to look back at Boy Miguel who nods his head in question as if to ask if they're going to meet later*

*She smiles, nods back then runs into the hotel*

*Boy Miguel is very pleased, smiles and punches the air. The punch should be timed so that it coincides with Pavarotti's very long last note*

### SCENE 3

*The scene opens twenty-four hours later. Open to some laid-back Spanish music. One set of sixties style suitcases is on the stage*

*When the Lights come up, Boy Miguel and Girl Lorna are standing far left against one of the arches. He has his left hand placed above her head allowing him to stand very close to her*

*Woman Regietta stands alone near the centre table. At her feet are her only belongings. They are not in a suitcase however but rolled very neatly in a blanket and tied*

**Boy Miguel**  One more kiss, eh?
**Girl Lorna**  I don't want to go home, Miguel.
**Boy Miguel**  Sure you do.
**Girl Lorna**  No, I don't.
**Boy Miguel**  No, no you no cry. Señor Dougie he see eyes look wet he wonder what wrong. Please no tear, eh?
**Girl Lorna**  What will I do when I get home?
**Boy Miguel**  Señor Dougie he must no know how you feel. (*Slight pause*) He tell me next week you move to new house. All women like new house.

**Girl Lorna**  I'd rather stay here with you.

*He cups her face in his hands and kisses her*

*Dougie comes out of the hotel. He is carrying a modern suitcase. He puts it down not too far away from the others*

**Woman Regietta**  (*quite anxious* ) What we do now, señor?
**Dougie**  Don't worry.
**Woman Regietta**  All day Miguel he have chance to speak. To ask no go, you know? Bus come soon and still he no say nothing.
**Dougie**  He is cutting it a bit fine. I think it's time to put plan B into action.
**Woman Regietta**  Maybe this lie between us no good idea after all, eh?
**Dougie**  No—I'm sure we're almost there. I was talking to him this afternoon and I'm convinced we're (*he indicates with his finger and thumb* ) this close to cracking him and the fact that he hasn't hired any help is a great sign.
**Woman Regietta**  What about señora Lorna?
**Dougie**  Oh, no problem there. She's simmering very nicely.
**Woman Regietta**  (*not understanding* ) Señor?
**Dougie**  I've got her stewing in her own ...

*Woman Lorna comes out of the hotel. She is struggling to carry her very full suitcase*

*Both Dougie and Woman Regietta watch her as she places it next to Dougie's*

*Boy Miguel leaves through the arches*

*Girl Lorna is left alone*

**Woman Regietta**  Señor, you put with yours, eh? ( *She indicates her belongings* )

*Dougie picks them up and places them on top of his and Woman Lorna's cases*

**Dougie**  (*to Woman Lorna* ) Yes, I'll put them with Lorna's here. Got

everything?
**Woman Lorna** (*very intensely* ) There's only my flight bag to come.
**Dougie** Right.
**Woman Regietta** I all ready. I no forget nothing.
**Woman Lorna** It's only in reception.
**Dougie** (*after a pause* ) Well go and get it then!

*Woman Lorna storms off back inside the hotel*

(*He smiles at Woman Regietta* ) See what I mean? She's very strung up.
**Woman Regietta** I better get little one.
**Dougie** Go on then.

*She gets up and as she passes him he touches her on the shoulder*

Don't worry ... we'll crack Miguel somehow.

*Woman Regietta smiles, not at all sure. She exits inside hotel*

*Dougie watches her go*

*After Woman Regietta has disappeared, Girl Lorna moves* DL *as she speaks to him*

**Girl Lorna** Who would have thought two weeks could go so quick?
**Dougie** (*going to her* ) You've enjoyed it then ?
**Girl Lorna** (*nodding* ) Have you?
**Dougie** Oh I've enjoyed the rest.
**Girl Lorna** Do me a favour and don't say that to anyone when we get back home.
**Dougie** No, you know what I mean.
**Girl Lorna** I know exactly what you mean.
**Dougie** I can't wait to get home.
**Girl Lorna** Well you've got your new job, haven't you?
**Dougie** You've got something new too.
**Girl Lorna** I haven't forgotten.
**Dougie** I know a lot of women who would kill for a four bedroom semi.
**Girl Lorna** Big houses don't impress me. I could be happy as Larry as long as I'm with the right fella.

**Dougie** (*putting his arm around her* ) Thanks.

*A slight pause*

*Girl Lorna moves away slightly*

> *Woman Lorna comes back out with her flight bag. She puts it with the rest of the cases. There is an awkward pause*

**Dougie** Is there anything wrong?
**Girl Lorna** No.
**Dougie** Are you sure?
**Woman Lorna** ( *going to stand right of Dougie; intensely* ) Yes. I don't know about you but everything is hunky dory with me.
**Dougie** (*to Girl Lorna* ) You don't seem quite right.
**Woman Lorna** Oh, you've noticed.
**Girl Lorna** I'm just nervous about flying that's all. I'll get over it.
**Dougie** (*to Girl Lorna* ) Nothing else bothering you, is there?
**Woman Lorna** Not really. I mean my husband's left me for someone else, I'm going to have a divorce, go back to work, sell the house, find a flat, tell the kids, but apart from that everything's bloody marvellous.
**Dougie** (*slight pause; to Woman Lorna* ) That's all right then. (*He looks at his watch* ) The bus will be picking us up before long.

*Dougie starts off in the direction of the hotel*

> I'm going to make sure Regietta hasn't forgotten anything.
**Woman Lorna** (*calling after him* ) She shouldn't have. She's been packed since yesterday!

*He exits into the hotel*

*Woman Lorna watches Dougie exit*

*Girl Lorna is looking off to where Boy Miguel went a couple of minutes ago. Woman Lorna turns to see where Girl Lorna is looking*

**Woman Lorna** (*lighting a cigarette* ) I wish you could feel the way I do now.

**Girl Lorna** Why?

**Woman Lorna** As bad as you feel I feel worse.

**Girl Lorna** He said he was upsetting me so he's gone for a walk. Can you remember if he comes back in time to wave me off?

**Woman Lorna** It's not good to know everything.

**Girl Lorna** Wouldn't you like to know what's going to happen to you next?

**Woman Lorna** (*raising her voice*) I haven't got crystal balls. It'll take you twenty-five years to realize that Miguel hasn't got them either. If you know what's good for you, when Dougie asks you to come back here for your silver wedding, tell him to bugger off. (*A pause*) I just want to have one last check of the room. Make sure I haven't left anything.

**Girl Lorna** I'll come with you.

*They both walk towards the hotel together*

*Woman Regietta comes out of the hotel carrying the baby*

*She walks between Woman Lorna and Girl Lorna*

*Girl Lorna doesn't stop and exits into the hotel*

*Woman Lorna turns to look at Woman Regietta. Woman Regietta senses her gaze and turns round to look at her*

**Woman Lorna** Do you know what I'd have done if I were you?

*Woman Regietta shakes her head*

I'd have burnt his bloody boat.

*Woman Lorna drags intensely on her cigarette but before going into the hotel she throws Woman Regietta her lighter*

*Woman Regietta catches it. She turns to look at Woman Lorna but she has gone inside*

*A slight pause. Woman Regietta ignites the lighter and stares at its flame*

*After a moment or two Boy Miguel appears from one of the arches. He is obviously looking for Girl Lorna. He spots the luggage and goes to it crossing in front of Woman Regietta. After he passes her the flame of the lighter goes out. Boy Miguel is checking Girl Lorna's luggage*

*While he is doing this Girl Regietta comes out of the hotel, stands and watches him. She moves closer to him before she shouts his name*

**Girl Regietta** Miguel!

*Woman Regietta looks on as she remembers it all*

**Boy Miguel** Aahh. Why you do that — you always do that?
**Girl Regietta** (*shouting*) Yeah I frighten shit — I know. Why you here? You wait for her? For English woman?
**Boy Miguel** (*shouting*) I always take guest to bus.
**Girl Regietta** (*shouting*) You always take guest to secret place.
**Boy Miguel** (*shouting*) Who are you, my wife?
**Girl Regietta** (*a pause; touching his arm with the back of her fingers*) You ask, maybe I say "yes".
**Boy Miguel** Regietta never say yes.
**Girl Regietta** How you know?
**Boy Miguel** Miguel, he never no ask. S'cuse.

*Boy Miguel pushes past her. Girl Regietta hits him as he goes. He turns to her*

I go get passport. They no go home without, you know?

*He exits into the hotel*

**Girl Regietta** Miguel! Miguel!

*Girl Regietta follows him into the hotel*

*A pause. Woman Regietta sits at centre table*

*Man Miguel comes onto terrace from L. He sees Woman Regietta*

**Man Miguel** (*after some time* ) What you think?
**Woman Regietta** (*starting off into the hotel* ) I remember many year ago
... and know now you never love me.

*A pause*

**Man Miguel** You ready, eh?
**Woman Regietta** The bus come ten, fifteen minute.
**Man Miguel** (*slight pause* ) It's not too late, you know?
**Woman Regietta** For what?
**Man Miguel** (*going to her* ) To change mind.
**Woman Regietta** Why I do that?
**Man Miguel** I think maybe you no likeYstrad.
**Woman Regietta** If no go, how I know?

*A slight pause*

**Man Miguel** (*sitting next to her at the table, he puts his hand on hers* )
I look for you today.
**Woman Regietta** (*snatching her hand away* ) So ?
**Man Miguel** You no here for long time.
**Woman Regietta** ( *pretending to be choked* ) I say goodbye to children.
**Man Miguel** You no find hard do that?
**Woman Regietta** (*moving* DR. *Crocodile tears* ) Of course hard — I cry
all day.
**Man Miguel** (*following her* ) I live in Ystrad, I find hard too ... maybe you
stay I find hard ... you know?
**Woman Regietta** (*sharply* ) What you ask?
**Man Miguel** Nothing nothing, I no ask nothing.
**Woman Regietta** (*shouting* ) You want Regietta stay, why you no ask
Regietta stay?
**Man Miguel** OK, you stay?
**Woman Regietta** No! I go to Ystrad. (*A pause* ) Why you change mind?
You no get help, eh?
**Man Miguel** I get plenty help.
**Woman Regietta** But have to pay this time.
**Man Miguel** I say no 'cos want Regietta help.
**Woman Regietta** (*suspiciously* ) Why you want Regietta help?
**Man Miguel** You here long time.

**Woman Regietta** Tell why.
**Man Miguel** I use to you.
**Woman Regietta** Tell why.
**Man Miguel** I move things in kitchen — plenty room now.
**Woman Regietta** Tell why.
**Man Miguel** I love you! (*He closes his eyes and makes a face* )
**Woman Regietta** (*exploding* ) Why you tell now, eh? Bus come ten minute, you tell now.

*Dougie comes out of the hotel followed by Woman Lorna. He is now wearing a very small thin jacket*

*Woman Lorna crosses the back of the terrace and takes up a position* DL

**Dougie** ( *seeing Woman Regietta and Man Miguel* ) There you are!
**Woman Regietta** Ah ... señor Dougie.
**Dougie** (*to Regietta* ) All packed and ready then?
**Woman Regietta** Señor ... Miguel, he say he love me. For first time in thirty year he say he love me.
**Dougie** (*to Woman Regietta* ) Well it's a bit late, isn't it?

*Woman Regietta nods in agreement*

**Man Miguel** Better to say now than never, eh?
**Dougie** (*to Man Miguel* ) It's not going to change anything. (*To Woman Regietta* ) I mean we still love each other, don't we?
**Woman Regietta** Of course.
**Man Miguel** I want she stay.
**Dougie** Why should she? I can offer her a lot more than this.
**Man Miguel** Like what, señor?
**Dougie** I want to marry her.
**Man Miguel** ( *slight pause* ) I want to marry too.
**Woman Regietta** You do?
**Dougie** He's just saying that, Regietta.
**Man Miguel** No, no, I mean.
**Dougie** I know you're mean. You won't even pay her for working here.
**Man Miguel** Of course I pay.
**Woman Regietta** You will?
**Dougie** Don't listen to him.

**Man Miguel** You stay, we come to special 'rrangement.
**Woman Regietta** I stay; we marry *and* pay wages?
**Man Miguel** Sure.
**Dougie** He's just telling you all this to change your mind.
**Woman Regietta** You right, I come to Ystrad.
**Man Miguel** Everything I say 'tis true.
**Dougie** I'll make her very happy.
**Man Miguel** Regietta happy here.
**Dougie** You think so? How can she be happy when you take women to your secret place?

*He looks at Woman Lorna who looks away*

**Man Miguel** I no do so more.
**Woman Regietta** You won't ?
**Man Miguel** I sell boat, you know?
**Woman Regietta** You promise?
**Man Miguel** Cross heart. (*He puts his right hand on the right side of his chest, then immediately changes to the left side so that his hand is now covering his heart* )
**Woman Regietta** I like believe, but ...
**Dougie** Miguel tells lies.
**Woman Regietta** True—I come to Ystrad.
**Man Miguel** No, no I will sell boat ... I give word.
**Woman Regietta** (*slight pause* ) So ... you say you love me.
**Man Miguel** Sure.
**Woman Regietta** You promise get married?
**Man Miguel** Get married.
**Woman Regietta** Pay wages.
**Man Miguel** Pay wages.
**Woman Regietta** Sell boat?
**Man Miguel** ( *swallowing hard* ) Sell boat.
**Woman Regietta** (*a pause* ) OK. I stay.

*Man Miguel is delighted. He kisses Woman Regietta's cheek several times. A slight pause*

Señor Dougie, you understand, eh?
**Dougie** Well, I'm devastated of course.

**Woman Regietta**  Miguel, he new man now, eh?

**Dougie**  I'm not all that sure so ... you'd better take this just in case. (*He takes a plane ticket out of his pocket* )

**Man Miguel**  What is paper?

**Dougie**  It's Regietta's air ticket. It's valid for three months. (*To Regietta*) Now if he doesn't do all he's promised — use it.

**Woman Regietta**  Ah you very nice man, you know?

**Man Miguel**  ( *resentfully* ) Very nice.

**Woman Regietta**  You're a *very*  nice man.

**Woman Lorna**  (*almost spitting it out* ) A *very, very*  nice man!

**Man Miguel**  I take inside, eh? (*He goes to pick up her belongings* )

**Woman Regietta**  (*to Dougie* ) Miguel, he new man, señor.

**Man Miguel**  (*holding Regietta's clothes* ) I put in old room, eh? You no go back to third floor.

*He goes into the hotel*

**Woman Regietta**  (*to Dougie* ) I sorry if I hurt you, señor. ( *She gives an exaggerated wink* )

**Dougie**  I understand. I've never been any competition for Miguel. (*He says this for Woman Lorna's benefit* )

**Woman Regietta**  (*turning to move nearer Woman Lorna* ) Miguel always look for woman of dreams. He no know I here all time. (*She gives a quick look in Dougie's direction* ) Often we look for something and all time 'tis there for us to see.

*She smiles at Dougie as she passes him and goes into the hotel*

*He turns and watches her exit*

**Woman Lorna**  (*slight pause* ) I can't believe what I've just heard.

**Dougie**  What do you mean?

**Woman Lorna**  For someone who's made you happier than you've ever been, you've taken it very well that she's decided to stay. It looks for all the world to me like it was a big set up.

**Dougie**  Well at least it got the pair of *them*  together.

**Woman Lorna**  And us?

**Dougie**  Oh I'm not sure where it leaves us.

**Woman Lorna**  (*after a slight pause* ) I just want to say one thing, Dougie, and then I'll leave the ball in your court. ( *Slight pause* ) I think you and me have hit rock bottom but the only way to go from here is up. We can divorce and get there on our own ... or we can try and work it out together. For what it's worth I'd rather try and sort it out between us. (*Slight pause* ) What do you say?

**Dougie**  We've got an awful lot of work to do.

**Woman Lorna**  I'm game.

**Dougie**  That's always good for starters.

**Woman Lorna**  (*slight pause* ) About Miguel——

**Dougie**  ( *interrupting* ) If we're going to stand any sort of chance, we've got to set down the ground rules — and that means no more talk of Miguel or Regietta, OK?

**Woman Lorna**  I just wanted to say—

**Dougie**  There's no need.

*Dougie puts his hand on Woman Lorna's arm. Very soft Spanish music plays*

There's really no need.

*Woman Lorna and Dougie kiss*

*Girl Lorna comes out of the hotel*

*Woman Lorna breaks away from Dougie as she holds back a tear*

*Girl Lorna finds it harder to do the same thing*

Are you upset?

**Woman Lorna**  (*still fighting it* ) No.

**Dougie**  (*to Woman Lorna* ) Yes, you are.

**Girl Lorna**  (*moving to stand on Dougie's right* ) No I'm not. I'm really not.

**Dougie**  (*to Woman Lorna* ) Everything's going to be OK, you know?

**Girl Lorna**  Is it?

**Woman Lorna**  I've made such a fool of myself.

**Dougie**  It happens to us all.

**Girl Lorna**  (*after a slight pause* ) Dougie?

*Dougie turns to her*

**Woman Lorna** (*screaming at Girl Lorna*) No! (*Very deliberately*) Don't
you say anything. (*Eventually she shakes her head as she turns away
slightly; slight pause*) I nearly told you all about it the last night of our
honeymoon. If that bus had been a couple of minutes late I might just
have come out with it.
**Dougie** (*to Woman Lorna*) Are you ready to go home?

*Woman Lorna nods*

**Girl Lorna** I suppose so.
**Dougie** (*to Girl Lorna*) You don't sound very sure.
**Girl Lorna** (*not meaning a word*) Of course I'm ready. I've had enough
of the plumbing here anyway. I can't wait to move into our new house.
**Dougie** (*to Girl Lorna as he puts his arm around her shoulder*) Do you
know something? I think we're going to be OK.
**Girl Lorna** (*unsure*) Are we?
**Woman Lorna** (*putting her two hands on Dougie's left shoulder; very
positively*) Yes, I'm sure of it.

*The coach is heard pulling up some distance away. The horn toots several
times*

*Dougie parts with Woman Lorna and Girl Lorna*

*Spanish music stops*

**Dougie** Ah, that's the bus.

*Woman Regietta and Man Miguel rush out of the hotel*

**Man Miguel** Aaahh 'tis here. You ready go, eh?

*Man Miguel catches hold of Dougie and kisses him on each cheek then
turns to do the same to Woman Lorna*

*Woman Regietta and Dougie kiss each other on the cheek. Immediately
they part. Woman Regietta sees Man Miguel kissing Woman Lorna*

*several times too many. She screams at him*

**Woman Regietta** Miguel!

*They spring apart*

**Dougie** I'd better take the cases to the bus.

*He picks up their cases and exits*

*An awkward pause*

**Man Miguel** You have safe journey home, eh?
**Woman Lorna** I hope so. *(Slight pause )* I er ... ( *She doesn't know what to say* )
**Woman Regietta** S'OK, señora. Nobody need say nothing. Come Miguel—we wave to bus, eh?

*Woman Regietta and Man Miguel go off in the direction of the bus*

*This leaves Girl Lorna and Woman Lorna alone on stage. They look at each other and soft Spanish music starts up again*

*Eventually Woman Lorna turns to leave and then stops to have one last look at her past. She blows Girl Lorna a kiss with one finger before running off*

*Girl Lorna is alone for a brief moment*

*Boy Miguel comes out of the hotel with two passports in his hand. He sees Girl Lorna standing there alone. He waits until she looks up at him. He opens his arms offering her one last hug*

*Just as they are about to embrace Dougie comes back out onto the terrace*

**Dougie** Yes the bus is ours. *(To Girl Lorna )* Sure now you haven't left anything behind?

*Girl Lorna doesn't answer him. A slight pause*

Right, well that's it then.
**Boy Miguel** Have safe journey, señor.

*He kisses Dougie on either cheek after which he hands him the passports*

Maybe come back next year, eh?
**Dougie** Maybe, I'm not sure. (*Slight pause* ) Er ... where's Regietta?
**Boy Miguel** Who know? Shall I say goodbye to her for you?
**Dougie** Please, yes. (*Another awkward pause. To Girl Lorna* ) Right. Well fit then.

*She smiles but makes no attempt to leave*

(*Slight pause* )Well I'll get these on. (*He picks up the cases* )
**Boy Miguel** You take good care señor!

*Dougie struggles off with the luggage, but before actually disappearing out of sight he turns to see if Girl Lorna is following him. She isn't*

*Boy Miguel waves to him. Dougie nods then looks at Girl Lorna*

*The bus toots again and Dougie exits*

*A pause. Boy Miguel doesn't turn round to look at Girl Lorna. After a moment she walks past him on her way out. He stops her by speaking to her*

**Boy Miguel** You too, señora.

*Girl Lorna stops, turns and runs to him. He cups her face in his hands*

Please, no tear, eh? Señor Dougie he no know why you cry. (*He wipes away her tears with his thumb* ) 'Tis very sad to see beautiful woman cry.

*She grabs hold of him and squeezes him to her*

*After a moment he holds her away from him, looks into her eyes and kisses her*

*Girl Regietta steps just outside of the hotel. She watches them*

*Just at the end of the kiss, Girl Lorna breaks away and runs off towards the bus*

*Boy Miguel has his back towards Girl Regietta. After a moment he turns and sees her*

**Girl Regietta** (*crying*) Why you do that? You always do that. You break my heart, you know?

*She turns to go back inside the hotel*

**Boy Miguel** (*shouting after her*) Regietta? (*Louder*) Regietta!

*She stops on top step. He takes her by the arm and brings her down to ground level. He kisses her several times all over her face*

You like to come to secret place?

*He takes her by the hand and walking backwards across the terrace, leads her off*

We swim in moonlight. Water very calm tonight.

*He now manoeuvres her so that she is in front of him and he is guiding her from behind*

You like moon? I like moon. Moon very sexy.

*She disappears through the arch*

*Boy Miguel looks out to the audience, smiles and winks and goes through the arch*

*Suddenly we hear the sound of the coach revving up and pulling off. There are adlibs of 'goodbye', 'take care', 'safe journey', etc. from Man Miguel and Woman Regietta. There are a couple of cheers then a slight pause*

*Man Miguel and Woman Regietta come back onto the terrace*

*Man Miguel begins to fold chairs and lean them against the empty tables. Woman Regietta is at another table doing the same*

**Woman Regietta** How many people we have come stay tomorrow?

**Man Miguel** I no sure. (*He takes a letter out of his pocket and hands it to her* ) Read letter. Six maybe, eh? Perhaps better have more table. What think? Two? Three, maybe?

**Woman Regietta** (*reading the letter*) They all lady who stay here nineteen-seventy. They say in letter still all work in same place together — how you say this word? (*She shows him the letter* )

**Man Miguel** (*hesitantly* ) Polikoff?

**Woman Regietta** Polikoff. Lady who write say they arrive in afternoon (*She reads part of the letter* ) "We are due to land at one thirty. Should be with you within the hour. We all looking forward to seeing you again, love Lena"

*Man Miguel almost catches his hand in a chair he is folding*

**Woman Regietta** (*screaming*) You know this 'Lena'.

**Man Miguel** Of course I no know.

**Woman Regietta** You keep photo, maybe.

**Man Miguel** What matter, eh? You think I try take to secret place?

**Woman Regietta** (*waving her plane ticket in front of him*) You promise you no never do no more.

**Man Miguel** Of course I promise. (*Slight pause* )You no believe Miguel, eh?

**Woman Regietta** (*slight pause as she eyes him up* )You leave for now.(*Referring to the chairs* ) Finish in morning. (*She puts the plane ticket down on the table, takes Man Miguel's hand and leads him to the hotel* )

*Without Woman Regietta seeing him, Man Miguel picks up the plane ticket and puts it in his pocket*

We go inside — lay ... in bedroom. (*She crosses the terrace* ) We look for 'match' together. (*Sexily* ) Maybe no damp no more, eh?

**Man Miguel** (*keenly*) Sure.
**Woman Regietta** You go room. Wait for me. I make look nice for you.
**Man Miguel** (*smiling*) We 'cook' together? Light oven, maybe? (*He shouts*) Strike match set fire to heart.

*Woman Regietta pushes Man Miguel inside the hotel and shouts after him*

**Woman Regietta** You set fire to heart. ( *Now alone outside the hotel* ) Regietta know something else she like to 'burn'.

*She laughs, ignites lighter and then runs off in the direction of the secret place*

*A couple of bars of aggressive Spanish music*

CURTAIN

# FURNITURE AND PROPERTY LIST

## ACT I
### SCENE 1

*On stage*:   Four or five tables, each with an umbrella. *On one*: glass of wine
        Six or eight folding chairs

*Off stage* :  Two glasses of wine (**Boy Miguel**)
        An open bottle of 'San Miguel' beer (**Man Miguel**)

*Personal* :  **Woman Lorna** : cigarettes and lighter
        **Boy Miguel**: cigarettes
        **Man Miguel**: handkerchief
        **Dougie**: wallet. *In it*: photograph

## ACT I
### SCENE 2

*Strike* :    Two glasses of wine, bottle of 'San Miguel' beer

*On stage*:   Tables. *On each*: teapot and cups
        On **Woman Lorna's** table: postcards, packet of cigarettes and lighter, full teapot, cups
        On **Girl Lorna's** table : postcards

*Off stage* :  Tray (**Girl Regietta**)
        Small tray. *On it:* tea things (**Woman Regietta**)
        Baby (**Woman Regietta**)
        Packet of cigarettes and box of matches (**Boy Miguel**)
        Camera in a case (**Dougie**)
        Duster (**Woman Regietta**)
        Tray: *On it*: Two glasses of wine (**Woman Regietta**)

*Personal* :  **Girl Lorna**: sunglasses
        **Woman Lorna**: sunglasses, bag. *In it*: Two photos

## ACT II
### Scene 1

| | |
|---|---|
| *Set* : | Tables. *On each* : lit candles, various drinks |
| *Off stage* : | Tray. *On it* : Harvey Wallbanger and pint of lager (**Woman Regietta**)<br>Long drink (**Man Miguel** ) |
| *Personal* : | **Girl Regietta:** Red rose<br>**Woman Regietta:** Red rose<br>**Man Miguel:** Wad of notes |

## ACT II
### Scene 2

| | |
|---|---|
| *Strike* : | Candles,various drinks |
| *On stage* : | Breakfast things on tables<br>Well-packed beach-bag at **Girl Lorna's** table<br>Baby (**Woman Regietta**)<br>Pair of shoes (**Woman Lorna**) |
| *Off stage* : | Tray (**Boy Miguel**)<br>Tray. *On it*: Two glasses of beer (**Man Miguel**)<br>Bottle of wine (**Boy Miguel**) |
| *Personal* : | **Woman Lorna:**Cigarettes<br>**Dougie:**Sunglasses<br>**Couple at table:**Money |

## ACT II
### Scene 3

| | |
|---|---|
| *Strike* : | Breakfast things, beach-bag |
| *On stage* : | One set of sixties style suitcases<br>Rolled up blanket |

*Off stage*:   Modern suitcase (**Dougie**)
Very full suitcase (**Woman Lorna**)
Flight bag (**Woman Lorna**)
Baby (**Woman Regietta**)
Two passports (**Boy Miguel**)

*Personal*:   **Woman Lorna**: Cigarettes and lighter
**Dougie**: Plane ticket
**Man Miguel**: Letter
**Dougie**: Brochure, handkerchief
**Man Miguel**: Wallet. *In it*: photo

# LIGHTING PLOT

Property fittings required: nil
Exterior. The same throughout

ACT I, Scene 1 Night

*To open*: A dim light from inside the ground floor of the hotel. Full moon effect on terrace. Small lights twinkling on the far side of the bay

| | | |
|---|---|---|
| *Cue* 1 | Introductory music ends<br>*Fade lights to black-out* | (Page 1) |
| *Cue* 2 | Black-out<br>*Bring lights up to above effect* | (Page 1) |
| *Cue* 3 | **Boy Miguel**: "We share wine together."<br>*A light comes on in an upstairs room in the hotel* | (Page 4) |
| *Cue* 4 | All three turn upstage to look at the full moon<br>*General lighting changes putting three in the<br>  smallest spot possible* | (Page 17) |
| *Cue* 5 | Very dramatic Spanish chords play<br>*Black-out* | (Page 17) |

Act I, Scene 2 Morning

*To open* : General lighting

| | | |
|---|---|---|
| *Cue* 6 | **Dougie**: " I remember."<br>*Lighting changes so that* **Dougie** *and* **Girl Regietta**<br>  *are in spot* | (Page 40) |
| *Cue* 7 | **Woman Regietta** stops **Dougie**<br>*Revert back to general lighting* | (Page 40) |

*Cue* 8     A bar or two of aggressive Spanish music          (Page 41)
            *Black-out*


ACT II, Scene 1 Morning

*To open*: General lighting

*Cue* 9     At end of Scene                                    (Page 55)
            *Fade to Black-out*


ACT II, Scene 2  Late evening

*To open* : General lighting

*No cues*


ACT II, Scene 3 Morning

*To open* : Black-out

*Cue* 10    Laid-back Spanish music                           (Page 67)
            *Lights up*

# EFFECTS PLOT

## ACT I

Cue 1    To open                                              (Page 1)
*Introductory music. Cut when ready*

Cue 2    Lights up on terrace                                 (Page 1)
*Two waves crashing in the distance*

Cue 3    **Woman Lorna:** " ... I remember". A pause          (Page 2)
*Slow lilting Spanish music*

Cue 4    **Boy Miguel** makes his way over to **Girl Lorna**  (Page 2)
*Reduce volume of music*

Cue 5    **Boy Miguel** goes inside the hotel                 (Page 4)
*Music swells but then suddenly stops*

Cue 6    A string of Spanish is heard                         (Page 4)
*China is heard smashing*

Cue 7    **Dougie** and **Man Miguel** sit with their eyes closed (Page 10)
*Soft Spanish music is heard*

Cue 8    **Man Miguel** : "Of course. Of course."             (Page 11)
*Fade music*

Cue 9    **Woman Lorna:** "I can see you now—"                (Page 12)
*Spanish music plays*

Cue 10   **Dougie:** "Didn't we Lorna?"                       (Page 12)
*The music stops*

Cue 11   **Woman Lorna:** "... as I can remember"             (Page 16)
*Spanish music plays*

Cue 12   **Boy Miguel** turns to **Girl Lorna**               (Page 17)
*The music stops*